Booker T. Washington:
A Re-Examination

Compiled by
Lee H. Walker

Edited by
Diane Carol Bast
S.T. Karnick

June 2008

Booker T. Washington:
A Re-Examination

Published by The Heartland Institute
19 South LaSalle Street #903
Chicago, Illinois 60603
phone 312/377-4000
fax 312/377-5000
www.heartland.org

Additional copies of this book
are available from The Heartland Institute
for the following prices:

1-10 copies	$5.95 per copy
11-50 copies	$4.95 per copy
51-100 copies	$3.95 per copy
101 or more	$2.95 per copy

Printed in the United States of America
ISBN-13 978-1-934791-02-8
ISBN-10 1-934791-02-4

Manufactured in the United States of America

(from left) Robert C. Ogden, a New York philanthropist; U.S. Secretary of War William H. Taft; Booker T. Washington; and industrialist Andrew Carnegie at the 25th anniversary of Tuskegee Institute (University) in 1906. *Library of Congress image LC J694-353A*

Contents

Part 1
Is Booker T. Washington Relevant Today?

Part 2
The Man and the Legacy

Part 3
Entrepreneurship and Economic Development

Part 4
Toward a More Accurate History

Part 5
Left, Right, and Black

Part 6
Self-Reliance and the Role of Government

PREFACE

Joseph L. Bast[1]

Since 2002, The Heartland Institute has shared office space with The New Coalition for Economic and Social Change, a "black think tank" led by Lee H. Walker. It is a unique and very productive partnership whereby Heartland's work gets a better hearing in the black community while The New Coalition's work benefits from our professional staff and access to resources.

The New Coalition traces its history to a conference convened by Dr. Henry Lucas and Dr. Thomas Sowell in 1980 in San Francisco, California. This conference, called the Fairmont Conference, attracted Democrats, Republicans, independents, and community activists from around the country. Together, they called for a New Black Agenda that stressed free enterprise, community, and individual empowerment.

Lee Walker has long dreamed of holding another conference that would capture the energy and excitement of the original Fairmont Conference, featuring a new generation of scholars and activists. In June 2006, with the enthusiastic help of Heartland's staff and supporters, Lee's dream became a reality.

The Symposium

Booker T. Washington: A Re-Examination was a two-and-a-half-day symposium examining every aspect of the life of a truly great American. Prominent academics from across the country came to Chicago to discuss Booker T. Washington's life and legacy. More than 20 individuals spoke at venues ranging from an auditorium on Northwestern University's downtown campus to meals at the DuSable Museum of African American History and on Lake Michigan aboard *The Spirit of Chicago*.

The result was an extraordinary event – the biggest gathering of academics and activists who support Booker T. Washington's agenda of education, entrepreneurship, and character development since the 1980 Fairmont Conference. We experienced debate as well as agreement, and a

---

[1] Joseph L. Bast is president of The Heartland Institute.

learning experience for speakers as well as their audiences.

The symposium has broken new ground in the effort to build a contemporary movement to advance what Lee Walker has aptly titled "The New Agenda." The New Agenda contains messages that resonate with large majorities of nonwhites and whites alike. It does not deny the history or reality of racism, yet it rises above the class warfare rhetoric and victimology of many nonwhite spokespersons and the often tone-deaf proclamations on the black situation by whites. It offers solutions, not just complaints, excuses, and blame, to people who are trying to climb society's ladder to personal and economic success. It has deep roots in the black intellectual tradition.

This book, containing the presentations and papers submitted at the symposium, is the first installment of an aggressive and long-overdue educational campaign. The symposium has provided essential content for that campaign, in the form of short essays, longer papers, and short and long DVDs for classroom use and for broadcast on cable and public television.

What a Think Tank Should Do

All of this, I'm happy to say, is exactly what a "think tank" such as The Heartland Institute should be doing. We're challenging old ways of thinking, creating a forum for the best and brightest minds, and reaching out to audiences who could benefit most from the ideas being discussed.

This book and the event that made it possible will make a lasting contribution to the debate over public policy and political philosophy, particularly as they affect the black community. It will also change forever many of the people who attended.

INTRODUCTION

Lee H. Walker[2]

The June 2006 symposium, convened for the specific purpose of reviving Washington's legacy, was the fruit of 10 years' labor. When I initially proposed the idea, I could not find five scholars interested in Booker T. Washington. The 22 academics and community leaders present at the symposium, however, bore witness to the renewed interest in Booker T. Washington among scholars, both black and white.

I believe the symposium was the largest gathering of intellectuals to celebrate and discuss the ideas of Booker T. Washington since his premature death in 1915. These scholars discussed many different aspects of Washington's life story, reexamined his contributions to black social advancement, and explored the relevance of his teachings to contemporary society.

I was especially honored by the presence of Margaret Washington Clifford, Booker T. Washington's granddaughter and oldest living descendent, at the symposium. Although she did not contribute a paper for this collection, she shared some fascinating personal stories at the symposium about growing up in the shadow of Tuskegee.

Although many today have never heard of him, the Wizard of Tuskegee was, without doubt, the most powerful and influential black leader of his time, and arguably of all time. He received honorary degrees from Harvard University and Dartmouth University, dined with U.S. Presidents and the Queen of England, and was the first black person to have his image appear on a U.S. stamp and commemorative coin. President Dwight D. Eisenhower created a national monument to Booker T. Washington in 1956.

Louis Harlan spent 25 years pouring over the Washington Papers collected in the Library of Congress before publishing his two-volume biography of Washington. Harlan won a Pulitzer Prize for his work, the first time a biography of a black had ever been so honored. When we recall that Washington began his life as a slave, his meteoric rise to greatness becomes

---

[2] Lee H. Walker is president of The New Coalition for Economic and Social Change and a senior fellow of The Heartland Institute.

even more remarkable.

In selecting scholars for the Booker T. Washington Symposium, I received considerable assistance from my associate, friend, and long-time collaborator Joseph L. Bast. Bast is president of The Heartland Institute, a free-market think tank based in Chicago. He shares my high regard for Booker T. Washington and contributed his time and resources to help make this event possible. I am deeply grateful for the help, encouragement, and support of Joseph Bast and The Heartland Institute.

Washington Was a Hero

At this stage of my life I am down to two main hobbies, golf and reading. Although I find myself golfing less these days, I hope to keep reading until I make my "final transition."

In the course of my studies, I once read that a hero is "someone of whom we can say that if they had not lived when they did, or acted as they did, the history of this country and the world would have been profoundly different." Although I am not a historian in the true sense – my degree was in economics, not history – I believe Booker T. Washington fits the definition. He was one of the most famous, influential, and respected men of his time, and perhaps of all time, either black or white. William Dean Howell, widely regarded as the Dean of American Letters, described Washington as "a public man second to no other American in importance."

Regarding Washington's famous speech at the Atlanta Exposition, Dr. Rayford W. Logan, head of history at Howard University, wrote in his book, *The Betrayal of the Negro from Rutherford B. Hayes to Woodrow Wilson*, "Booker T. Washington's speech in Atlanta, Georgia on September 18, 1895 was one of the most effective pieces of political oratory in the history of the United States. It deserves a place alongside that in which Patrick Henry proclaimed, 'Give me liberty, or give me death.'"

Clark Howell, editor of the *Atlanta Constitution*, praised the speech as "one of the most notable speeches ever delivered to a Southern audience." Pulitzer Prize winner David Levering Lewis counted Washington's speech as "one of the most consequential pronouncements in American history."

It is astounding that a man so widely respected and even revered by his contemporaries is now so thoroughly overlooked. What was it that made Booker T. Washington the central figure in American race relations at the dawn of the twentieth century? Why did historians of the era label the years 1895 to 1915, "The years of Washington?" And why have modern scholars been so quick to dismiss this mountain of a man? These questions and many others were addressed during the course of the symposium.

Washington's Social Philosophy

Washington leapt onto the national scene following the nationwide publication of his speech at the Atlanta Exposition in 1895. Perhaps it was fitting that 1895 was also the year famed abolitionist Frederick Douglass died. Douglass, one of Washington's personal heroes, had been black America's leader and spokesman for 50 years.

Although Washington became a very different type of leader, he inherited Douglass's firm belief in the strength and capability of his black brethren. When a white journalist had asked Douglass, "What do you blacks want from white people?" Douglass's well-known response was, "Just leave us alone and we can take care of ourselves." Washington likewise believed former slaves could stand on their own feet and achieve prosperity in American society.

In the years leading up to 1895, Washington earned a solid reputation by founding and directing Tuskegee Institute, now Tuskegee University. While the freedman's bureau had used northern white men to establish and run black schools such as Fisk, Howard, and Hampton, Washington was the first black to head up such a school.

As the principal of Tuskegee, teaching, fundraising, and managing the school consumed the majority of his time. However, after his 1895 speech at the Atlanta Exposition – the first time a black man had ever shared the stage with whites in the south – Washington assumed the mantle of black leadership from Douglass almost overnight. He became more than an educator; he became the hero and role model of his people.

Upon inheriting the mantle of leadership, Washington confronted the daunting challenge of transforming emancipated slaves into productive and prosperous citizens. The end of Reconstruction and the resurgence of violent white supremacy further complicated his mission. After running Tuskegee for 14 years, however, Washington had developed strong opinions about how blacks should pursue freedom and prosperity.

First and foremost, Washington advocated quality education for black children and adults. He understood that in the aftermath of slavery, freedmen needed schools that could teach them to read (something that was illegal under slavery) so they could develop the understanding and skills required of productive citizens. He founded the Tuskegee Institute in 1881, and for many years he quietly raised money from white philanthropists to fund new schools for blacks in the segregated South.

A second theme in Washington's life, closely tied to education, was self-reliance. Tuskegee University began as the Normal School in Tuskegee, Alabama and focused on training black men and women to become skilled at building, farming, and other occupations so they could earn their way into mainstream American society. Washington was convinced, as he wrote in *Up from Slavery* in 1901, that "the actual sight of a first-class house that a Negro has built is ten times more potent than pages of discussion about a house that he ought to build, or perhaps could build." (p. 113)

A third Washington theme was entrepreneurship. Living at a time of intense racism and segregation, Washington encouraged thousands of black men and women to look at the need for goods and services in their communities as an opportunity to start their own businesses. In 1900, Washington founded the first black businessmen's association – the National Negro Business League (NNBL). He personally helped many black businesses get started by introducing black entrepreneurs to white investors.

In 1901, Washington published his autobiography, *Up from Slavery,* which became the best-selling book ever written by a black. It was eventually translated into seven languages and was as popular in Europe as it was in Africa. *Up from Slavery* was more than an autobiography: It was a ringing endorsement of Washington's major themes: education, self-help, and entrepreneurship.

Clash with DuBois

Although Washington engaged the imagination and loyalty of blacks everywhere, especially in the South, he was not without critics. Washington's biggest antagonist during his lifetime was his one-time friend W.E.B. DuBois. Even though DuBois had requested a teaching position at Tuskegee several times – a request Washington repeatedly granted – DuBois eventually rejected Washington's social philosophy.

In 1903, DuBois published his book, *The Souls of Black Folk,* in which he criticized Washington and challenged him for leadership of the black race. DuBois also retracted his previous praise for Washington's speech at the Atlanta Exposition, dubbing it "The Atlanta Compromise." DuBois contended that without full political rights Washington's economic program would not help blacks achieve equality with whites.

After the publication of *The Souls of Black Folk*, blacks essentially divided into two camps, one loyal to Washington and the other to DuBois. Followers of Washington and DuBois continued to vie with each other (despite the fact that DuBois actually lessened his criticism of Washington later in life) following Washington's untimely death in 1915. Although subsequent black leaders overwhelmingly embraced DuBois's position, the debate over who speaks for black America continues today.

Washington's Ideas Today

The principal reason I convened the symposium is the firm conviction that the ideas of Booker T. Washington are even more relevant today than they were 150 years ago. When Washington was alive, there was intense opposition from whites to any effort to economically empower and educate the black community. Today, opposition is considerably less, and there is widespread interest in reducing the "achievement gap" between white and black students. Leaders in both the white and black community are also trying to increase black business creation.

Booker T. Washington is not as widely known today as he was in his time or in the decades following his death. Because he stressed self-improvement and economic advancement over the quest for political power, he was drawn into increasingly bitter debates with W.E.B. DuBois and others seeking immediate political equality for blacks. From the 1960s until the 1990s, there seemed to be little room in discussions of black ideology for a "conservative" like Washington. But this is changing, and it needs to change even more.

Having achieved political equality with whites, blacks have largely achieved the agenda set out by DuBois and his followers. The time seems right to discuss a New Agenda that can advance the black community, an agenda that will help blacks solve the problems that break up too many families and undermine economic security. In the words of Thomas Sowell, "The economic and social advancement of black Americans in this country is still a great unfinished task. The methods and approaches currently used for dealing with this task have become familiar over the past years and they demand reexamination."

If blacks are to achieve the fullness of the American Dream, we need to move beyond political agitation and re-embrace the agenda of Booker T. Washington: quality education, self-reliance, character, and entrepreneurship.

Conclusion

By promoting Booker T. Washington – the man as well as his ideas – we can attract the attention of millions of people who would otherwise not be interested in debating public policies. The 150th anniversary of Booker T. Washington's birth was the hook, so to speak, for engaging people in the debate about the next step forward for black Americans. I believe that if we embrace Washington's agenda, our future will be bright and our potential unlimited.

As Washington said, "At the bottom of education, at the bottom of politics, at the bottom of religion itself there must be for our race, as for all races ... economic independence."

PART 1

IS BOOKER T. WASHINGTON RELEVANT TODAY?

Chapter 1

Booker T. Washington Was Right

Anne Wortham[3]

As a member of the Tuskegee Institute class of 1963, I am truly a beneficiary of Booker T. Washington's legacy. I want to pay tribute to him, and to all the teachers and administrators who carried on the noble task of teaching and educating students like me.

The first thing I'd like to say is this: Booker T. Washington was right. I am the evidence. We can also see that he was right when we look at the consequences in the lives, systems, and communities in our country that have departed from the virtues and values that Washington argued constitute the necessary foundation of black progress.

One of Washington's well-known metaphors was, "Cast down your bucket where you are." That was a theme in his history-making speech at the Atlanta Exposition in 1895.

First, I want to offer a summary of what I think the metaphor means. I will then review developments in the thinking of black leaders that amounted to the rejection of Washington's approach to black advancement. Lastly, I will cite an instance of a graduate of Tuskegee Institute who has failed miserably to fulfill the responsibilities of his public office by exemplifying everything that is offensive to Booker T. Washington's legacy.

---

[3] Dr. Anne Wortham is associate professor of sociology at Illinois State University.

Understanding a Metaphor

"Cast down your bucket where you are." I first heard that statement from my dad. I don't know how he learned of it, as he was self-educated and certainly hadn't read Washington's works. It was just one of many character-building adages floating around in the small town environment in which I grew up.

But Washington's critics have distorted the metaphor to suggest that his words were those of an appeaser of white racism, an "Uncle Tom." It is wrongly used to suggest Washington believed the best approach to race relations was that blacks should not protest the system of white supremacy that blocked their strivings.

But if Washington actually believed that blacks should not protest the state of their community, why did he devote all of his life to promoting industrial education, economic self-sufficiency, self-responsibility, and self-cultivation? Those who often use the "cast down your bucket" metaphor to belittle his accomplishments and dismiss his ideas don't ask that question. By no means did Washington mean people should simply be satisfied with where they were.

Washington was himself an instrument of change as well as protest. "Cast down your bucket where you are" was a call to blacks as well as whites to do everything within their power to resist the forces of racism and contribute to the economic advancement of the south. The parable Washington told, in which the metaphor was made, makes its meaning quite clear. Let me quote the parable as he told it.

> A ship lost at sea for many days suddenly sighted a friendly vessel. From the mast of the unfortunate vessel was seen a signal: "Water, water. We die of thirst." The answer from the friendly vessel at once came back: "Cast down your bucket where you are." A second time, the signal, "Water, send us water!" went up from the distressed vessel. And was answered: "Cast down your bucket where you are." A third and fourth signal for water was answered: "Cast down your bucket where you are." The captain of the distressed vessel, at last heeding the injunction, cast down his bucket and it came up full of fresh, sparkling water from the mouth of the Amazon River.

Washington followed the story with the lessons he meant his audience to take from it.

> To those of my race who depend on bettering their condition in a foreign land, or who underestimate the importance of preserving friendly relations with the southern white man who is their next door neighbor, I would say: "Cast down your bucket where you are." Cast it down, making friends in every manly way of the people of all races, by whom you are surrounded.

To those of the white race who look to the incoming of those of foreign birth and strange tongue and habits for the prosperity of the South, were I permitted, I would repeat what I have said to my own race: "Cast down your bucket where you are." Cast it down among the eight millions of Negroes whose habits you know, whose fidelity and love you have tested in days when to have proved treacherous meant the ruin of your fireside. Cast down your bucket among these people who have without strikes and labor wars tilled your fields, cleared your forests, builded your railroads and cities, brought forth treasures from the bowels of the earth, just to make possible this magnificent representation of the progress of the South.

Calling for Self-Reliance

Clearly Washington used this adage to impress upon black and white Southerners that between them, they possessed the resources with which to create prosperity in the region. That they should rely on each other was all the more pressing in the face of the South's lag behind the economies of the northern and the midwestern states, where industrialization was intensifying. Remember, the year was 1895, when there was widespread anticipation of a changing labor force as European immigrants poured into the country.

In the timespan between 1881, when Tuskegee was established, and 1920 – five years after Washington's death in 1915 – nearly 23.5 million souls arrived from southern and eastern Europe, especially from Austro-Hungary, Italy, and Russia. Although the immigrants were white, they were strangers in the land, whereas black and white southerners knew each other intimately ... *very* intimately. The key to each other's well-being, and the key to the economic competitiveness of the agricultural South with the industrial North, was staring them in the face. *It was in each other.*

As we know, it was not until the South was forced to abandon Jim Crow laws and a generation of moderate whites took the reins of political and economic power in the South, that the South indeed finally began to become competitive.

"Cast down your bucket" was the advocacy not of resignation or passive accommodation, but of self-initiated and self-responsible action. At the 1922 unveiling of the Booker T. Washington memorial, Dr. George Cleveland Hall said of Washington in this regard, "He changed a crying race to a trying race and put in their hands the wonderful crafts of the age. He instilled in their minds the dignity of labor and urged them to stop marking time, but keep pace with the grand march of civilization."

"Cast down your bucket where you are" is a methodology of progress, not of passivity and stagnation. Passivity is the abdication of responsibility. Washington was exhorting blacks and whites to get on with doing what was necessary to bring about their mutual advancement. His message was the equivalent of: "Here you are, each of you has resources, you *are* the bucket; cast it down within each other."

Washington's call for self-reliance and self-responsibility entails an acknowledgment of every human being's fundamental responsibility toward existence itself, to respect facts and not allow one's perception of the facts to be overridden by his or her wishes.

Washington was emphatic in his belief that freedom entails the responsibility to accept facts. He wrote, "I have a great faith in the power and influence of facts. It is seldom that anything is permanently gained by holding back a fact."

Recognizing Reality

One fact that Washington refused to evade, and acknowledged in many speeches, was that despite the difficulties created by racism, there was no better place in which to freely invest one's sweat and toil than the United States. He explicitly states this conviction in *Up from Slavery*: "When we look at the facts, we must acknowledge that notwithstanding the cruelty and moral wrong of slavery, the 10 million Negroes inhabiting this country who themselves or whose ancestors went through the slavery, are in a stronger and more hopeful condition materially, intellectually, morally, and religiously than is true of any equal number of black people in any other portion of the globe. This I say not to justify slavery, but to call attention to a fact and to show how Providence so often uses men and institutions to accomplish a purpose."

For Washington, to refuse to acknowledge facts, even uncomfortable ones, is essentially irresponsible, a principle he repeatedly pointed out to students at Tuskegee. During his Sunday evening talks in the college chapel, which are reproduced in his book, *Character Building*, he not only encouraged them, but often admonished them when they fell short of the standard of excellence in character, academic achievement, and productiveness.

Building Character

Another famous adage of Washington's is, "Character is power." Character, of course, is an individual's personal culture, and it *is* power. According to Washington, humiliating experiences of racial prejudice and discrimination do not absolve one from the responsibility of cultivating his or her character.

Talking to his students, Washington once said, "We want also to be sure that we remain simple in our dress and in all our outward appearance. I do not like to see a young man who is poor and whose tuition is being paid by someone and who has no books, sometimes has no socks, sometimes has no decent shoes, wearing a white stiff shiny collar which he has sent away to be laundered. I do not like to ask people to give money for such a young man as that."

Washington wanted the young man to learn that it was much better to learn to launder his collars himself than to pretend to be what he was not. As he explained to the student, "When you send a collar to the city laundry, it indicates that you have a bank account. It indicates that you have money ahead and can afford luxury. Now, I do not believe that you can afford it! And that kind of pretense and that kind of acting do not pay. Get right down to business, as I have said. If we [the student-run campus laundry] cannot do up your collars well enough to suit you, why, get some soap and water and start here and learn to launder your own collars."

There are numerous such lessons in *Character Building*. They are instructive and inspiring; and when I read them I hear my father issuing similar chastisements to his children for failing to maintain a sensible priority of values. When Washington spoke to the young man as he did, he understood his teaching to be directed toward instilling self-responsibility, the other side of political freedom, and both of which are anchored in human rationality. "Freedom is serious business," said Washington.

Telling the Truth

Washington's most influential critic was scholar and political activist W.E.B. DuBois, who demanded full social and political equality for blacks, and believed that despite Washington's efforts in opposition to racial injustice, by advising against "open agitation" he harmed the interests of blacks by creating the impression that the South was justified in its attitudes. In his book, *Dusk of Dawn*, DuBois also accused Washington of what is today called "blaming the victim." In his view, the emphasis Washington gave to "the short-comings of the Negro" in his public speeches was "interpreted widely as putting the chief onus for his condition upon the Negro himself."

But Washington saw no honor in pretending that blacks, or whites for that matter, were more culturally developed than they were. Moreover, acknowledgment of behavior that was detrimental to the improvement of black life and race relations was the necessary first step on the road toward those goals.

Rejection of Self-Help

It appears that the metaphor "cast down your bucket where you are" has been interpreted by many as the equivalent of the paradoxical adage, "pull yourself up by your own bootstraps." Although I have been unable to find evidence that Washington ever referred to the latter, which is impossible to do, it is generally understood that both expectations entail the virtues of self-reliance and self-responsibility.

Since Washington, few leaders in the black community have emphasized the connection between virtue and success. The most concerted opposition to Washington's philosophy of thrift, industry, and self-help, and his emphasis on the primacy of black economic development, was led by the National Association for the Advancement of Colored People (NAACP), founded in 1909, which espoused a program of public agitation for the Negro's full civil and political rights.

As Harold Cruse points out in *Plural But Equal* (1987), the NAACP's rejection of the programmatic primacy of black economic development over civil rights agitation was at odds with the reality of the high value Americans placed on property ownership, private enterprise, technological development, and industrial expansion. It also evaded the relationship of blacks to that reality. Thus, while European immigrants were responding to their exclusion with strategies of private-sector economic development in order to enter the economic mainstream, blacks were being advised by white liberals to reject programs of economic advancement.

In 1924 three hundred blacks from sixty-three organizations, led by Kelly Miller (1863-1939), dean of Howard University, met in Chicago to formulate a program that was more relevant to the situation of blacks and free of the ideological and financial control of liberals. According to Harold Cruse, in *Plural But Equal*, the overall programmatic policy of this national council of leaders, which reflected the philosophy of Booker T. Washington, was "to inaugurate on the large scale a ... period of self-help and organized cooperation directed toward discharging our share of responsibility, direction, and effort in the solution of the race situation in America."

Moved by the crippling impact of the Depression on the black community, and representing a contingent of the delegates at the NAACP's 1932 annual convention, the well-known black conservative journalist George Schuyler (1895-1977) urged the NAACP to "advance the colored people of this country" by organizing "a consumers' cooperative society in every city where it has a branch. ... The opportunity is now and has long been at hand. The time may soon come when this opportunity is past. By all means let us do something economically constructive before our people succumb to the forces making for their destruction." But Schuyler's plea went unheeded.

The Birth of Dependency

Immobilized by its policy of political activism, the NAACP was put in the position of relying on Roosevelt's New Deal as the "bountiful dispenser of black uplift." The result, writes Cruse, was that blacks were made "economic wards of the state." As such, "blacks born during the 1930s and beyond would become the 'Children of the New Deal,' indoctrinated with the psychology of dependency on the government."

Although Washington's influence had not entirely abated, it was not sufficient to motivate the black educated elite to revisit his message and gain some insight that might have led them to see the economic solution to the shattering blow of the Great Depression. "They had forgotten nothing, and had learned nothing," writes Cruse.

Now in the throes of the Depression, the NAACP and the New Deal succeeded in making the Negro problem the nation's problem and in shifting responsibility for the Negro's plight from the Negro's shoulder to anyone and everyone. This remains the operating policy of race relations policy to this day. Black leaders and their white allies have successfully institutionalized the designation of blacks as the perpetual victim; any expectation that blacks should be imbued with the virtues of self-help – thrift, discipline, patience, good manners, and productivity – is considered not only blaming the victim, but expecting the victim to embrace "white" values.

As Kevern Verney points out in *Art of the Possible: Booker T. Washington and Black Leadership in the United States, 1881-1925* (2001), "In ideological terms industrial education and the late nineteenth century mantra of self-help, which Washington's life and career so graphically personified, have long since lost the capacity to command universal support."

The emergence of Martin Luther King, Jr. and the civil rights movement of the late 1950s, led by the black middle-class, might have been a period when the black community might have led the nation in reaffirming the necessary connection of individual liberty and self-responsibility. King was aware of Washington's message and seemingly believed, as he wrote in his last book, *Where Do We Go From Here: Chaos or Community?* (1967), that "The Negro must not wait for the end of segregation that lies at the basis of his own economic deprivation. He must act now to lift himself up by his own bootstraps." But, as Cruse points out, King exerted his moral authority instead in the interest of "the brotherhood of man" and the redemption of America's soul. "King should have turned his moral authority back on the black minority itself, delivered a secular message of self-determination, and said in effect, 'get your own house in order.' Unfortunately, that was not King's message," writes Cruse.

Instead, in the last chapter of *Where Do We Go From Here?* King, relying on the ideas of John Kenneth Galbraith, advocated the guaranteed income as the way to abolish poverty. "Earlier in this century this proposal would have been greeted with ridicule and denunciation as destructive of initiative and responsibility," observed King. But that way of thinking, including the notion that poverty could be solved "by first solving something else," was "simplistic." With this characterization, King effectively dismissed Washington's abiding premise of the causal connection between virtue and the freedom to pursue and sustain economic well-being.

Distortion of the Legacy

After suffering decades of denigration as an appeaser and Uncle Tom, Washington's reputation and legacy were redrawn by scholars who portrayed him, not as the voluntary pluralist that he was, but as a separatist who could be an ally, at least in spirit, of Malcolm X, whose rallying cry was self-determination. The problem with this resurrection of Washington was that its proponents understood the "self" in self-determination to mean a collective racial self, and viewed the fate of the individual as dependent on the fate of the race as a whole.

This was a significant misreading of what Washington believed and advocated. It was not racial determination that was key in Washington's approach but the self-responsibility of individuals. In direct opposition to the scientific racism of his time, which promoted the proposition that race is destiny, Washington consistently argued that *character is destiny*. In his view the fate of the race, about which he cared deeply, depended on individuals. Only individuals possess the conscious awareness that is required to attain the virtues necessary for the uplift and advancement of the race. "Few things can help an individual more than to place responsibility on him, and to let him know that you trust him," argued Washington.

By the end of the twentieth century, the psychology of dependency, institutionalized by the welfare state, was being expressed by the politics of victimhood and its corollary, the postmodern tribalism of "identity politics." Well into the twenty-first century, the virtues that Washington espoused and that history has shown are the keys to human survival are rejected as the tricks and traps of elitism. And any black person who dares criticize fellow blacks is accused of "self-hatred" by blacks and whites alike. They believe their accusation is justified because the premise of their practice of identity politics is that the self is collective, not the autonomous possession of individuals. Indeed, the very idea of individual autonomy and other tenets of ethical individualism are defined by scholars as elements of "symbolic racism."

Insult to the Legacy

It was in this cultural climate that Hurricane Katrina touched down on the politically corrupt city of New Orleans in the dysfunctional state of Louisiana in a national society whose mainstream culture is in a state of regression. The raging waters of the Gulf Coast washed up the ultimate insult to Washington's legacy and the center of learning, to which he devoted his life: the incompetent, jive-talking paragon of arrogant victimhood, New Orleans mayor Ray Nagin, a 1973 graduate of Tuskegee Institute. And it was in his chronicle of Nagin's response to the hurricane's devastation that the widely-read and influential historian Douglas Brinkley delivered the crowning insult to Booker T. Washington's legacy.

In his book, *The Great Deluge*, Brinkley describes Nagin as "the glamorous CEO mayor, all hat and no cattle." In the belief that Nagin is in the pocket of the business community, Brinkley criticizes the mayor for being too much like Booker T. Washington. Nagin, he writes, is "all Booker T. Washington, pull yourself up by your bootstraps, with a touch of Hollywood for good measure." Then Brinkley doubles the insult by commenting, "There was little W.E.B. DuBois in his repertoire."

Nothing could be further from the truth. On the Saturday before the landfall of Hurricane Katrina, instead of employing city resources to evacuate vulnerable residents, Nagin spent the day worrying about whether the city's hotel owners were going to sue him or not. A black politician who is a puppet of commercial interests, as Brinkley portrays Nagin, cannot possibly be fairly compared to Booker T. Washington. In fact Nagin is everything that Washington thought was detrimental to black progress and to American civilization. The irony of Brinkley's defamation of Washington by linking him with Nagin is that throughout his intriguing book he presents numerous examples of Nagin doing exactly the opposite of what Washington would do.

As a nineteenth-century Victorian, Washington would never have so brazenly shirked the challenges of leadership and looked to the federal government, demanding to know "Where is the cavalry?" He would have prepared his government and the citizens of New Orleans for disaster long before Hurricane Katrina struck the Gulf. But Nagin, officials in his government, and those who elected him approach reality with a different mindset than Washington: They see nothing to be gained by casting down one's bucket where he is. And the idea that character is power is foreign to them. Hurricane Katrina revealed that for them and too many of their fellow Americans, power lies in victimhood.

What many Americans saw as the consequence of white racism, a few others saw as the exposed cancerous wound of the welfare state, the psychological collectivism that fuels it, and the bigotry of low expectations that justifies it. Although the mostly white parishes around New Orleans waited for help as long as the poorest wards did, two-thirds of blacks polled saw racism as a cause of the city government's failure to deliver quick relief. Although disaster preparedness and evacuation are the responsibilities of city, county, and state governments, citizens of New Orleans claimed that the federal government allowed people to die simply because of the color of their skin.

Evidence-free charges of racism by leaders in every sector of the society crowded out the voices of those who found the causes in New Orleans's poverty, its long history of incompetence and corruption, historically crooked police force, and long record of refusing to confront its vulnerability to a massive hurricane. In the face of plenty of warning, it was Ray Nagin who delayed the evacuation order, had no drivers ready to operate the school buses that stood idle, failed to stock the Superdome with food and water, and let looters rampage without any interference from police. Yet the world agreed with Rapper Kanye West's claim that Katrina victims were left for days without food and water because "George Bush doesn't care about black people." (At one point, according to a Google search, West's statement had been published more than 400,000 times.) And Nagin was dubbed a "folk hero."

The Dream Denied

When Booker T. Washington urged black and white southerners to cast down their bucket where it was, he was confident that slavery was in back of him and that before him was the potential to realize a prosperous region and nation of virtuous, self-reliant citizens enjoying the fruits of reason, productiveness and political equality. As the carrier of that hope he agreed with Frederick Douglass, that great apostle of liberty and celebrant of self-made men, that people are the "architects of their own good fortunes," that if given the chance, "the Negro will do whatever he can do well." Like Douglass, Washington and the moral reformers of his era were counting on the culture's capacity to sustain the nexus of reason, liberty, and virtue, and expected that their own heroic investment in human progress would inspire future generations of Americans to make possible the realization of the American dream.

Instead, by the time of Washington's death, the nation had already taken the first steps into the future on the road to serfdom. If it were possible for him to see the future, he would see that as the nation has proceeded down that road, its culture has regressed so far from the virtues of rationality and responsibility that the mere fact that Nagin and the majority of showcased Katrina victims were black was sufficient to unleash the transfer of responsibility from blacks to all whites and American institutions. He would no doubt recoil in indignation before the realization that helplessness has become the currency of success and power.

Chapter 2

What Manner of People Are We?

Glenn C. Loury[4]

I'm not going to pretend to be a historian of Booker T. Washington's legacy and his works. I am not. I am an economist – basically a numbers guy.

But some years ago, in the late 1970s, I was a young economist just out of graduate school, teaching at the University of Michigan in the shadow of Detroit. The civil rights movement was already over in the late 1970s, and it was obvious to anybody who was paying attention that it was over. The era of marches, protests, demonstrations, moral appeals, and leveraging off of the situation of African-Americans as victims of discrimination and unfair treatment, had run its course.

Yet the problems of incomplete development, inequality, and pathology were obvious. The problems of violence, the problems of disintegration of family, the problems of economic marginality, and the issues of globalization were already rearing their heads. You could see them from Ann Arbor, Michigan. Just over the ivory tower, one could see reality impinging on the steel and automobile industries. One could see that labor union leverage to get some part of the rents to this or that industry and to spread them around among the workers was dying out as a model of progress.

And one could see the "underclass," the intractable problems associated with behavioral pathology in the lower economic regions of the black community, rearing its ugly head.

Need for Stronger Families

So I became a neoconservative in those years. I was never really a liberal; I was just an MIT-trained economist who happened to be in Ann Arbor, Michigan. But because I was black, I think people assumed I was supposed to be a liberal.

---

[4] Dr. Glenn C. Loury is the Merton P. Stoltz Professor of Social Sciences in the economics department at Brown University.

But I looked around at what was happening and I read people such as James Q. Wilson, Nathan Glazer, and Daniel Patrick Moynihan, and I thought these guys were actually saying things that were relevant to the situation. I ask you to consider the implications for a community of the fact that two-thirds of the children are born to women who are not married, that there is no husband in the home, that the children are being raised by the mother alone.

This is not a moral statement that I'm making. I'm not passing judgment on anybody. I'm asking you to consider the implications for the development of human beings of the fact that within a community it would be the norm – and not only the norm, but twice as often as the opposite – that the child would be raised by a mother alone. After all, two incomes are more than one, and 48 hours a day of parental supervision is twice as much time as 24 hours a day of it. Both common sense and social science evidence refute the view that having a single parent is not a disability, a deficit, something that holds people back.

Now, when that demographic fact about life in the African-American community was unfolding itself in the years after World War II, there were people who were sounding the alarm in various ways, who were saying that this was going to be a problem which, if it was not overcome, all of this civil rights remonstration is going to mean nothing, because the breaking down of the barriers inhibiting the participation of African-Americans will not solve the problem if the capacities are not developed in human beings to seize the opportunities that are created by the lowering of those barriers. This is the problem of seizing the potentiality of freedom that Booker T. Washington talked so much about – this is not the problem of clearing an obstacle. It's the problem of taking advantage of what happens after the obstacle has been cleared, and this is a problem that is still with us.

Need for New Approach

When I was a young economist at the University of Michigan looking over at the city of Detroit, thinking about my hometown of Chicago, following the statistics, and looking at what was happening to black people in the new American economy, I was concerned that the civil rights formulation – the posture, the set of claims, the rhetoric, the political strategy, and the philosophy – was simply inadequate to the task. It was outmoded; it was not dealing with reality.

It was, in the first place, unmanly. It was a servile posture. And here I found something in Washington's writings to encourage my thinking in this regard. It was not straight-backed. It was not standing up straight. It was not taking responsibility for one's own condition. It was constantly being in the position of asking white people to do for us something which the very tone of the civil rights movement suggested wasn't going to happen.

The tone of the movement was that we are victims, they are racist, they don't care anything about us anyway, and America is racist. It was a self-contradictory attitude: Why would you ask your oppressor, the one who's holding you down, the one who has contempt for you, to pave your path ahead for you? Why would you rely upon your oppressor to deliver you from your condition? But that was how the argument went.

The defiant, straight-backed, proud, "manly," Booker T. Washington-oriented response to our condition had tremendous appeal for a young MIT-trained economist who wasn't quite signed on yet as an ACLU liberal. Why don't we get busy, I thought; why don't we cast down our buckets where we are? Why are the streets in front of our houses full of trash and broken glass when we could easily sweep them up ourselves? Why are our children ill-educated when we can educate them? Why is there so much crime in our community? Why is – just to take a random example – Congressman John Conyers so busy holding hearings on the Hill about police brutality when his own constituents can't get from their homes to their places of work or school without being savaged by criminals right there in his own community? And so on and so on and so on.

Need for New Politics

And so in the early 1980s I began writing essays with observations such as, "What with the world going the way it is, what with globalization, what with the obvious end of Johnson-era Great Society politics, and what with all the problems besetting the black community, how can we still be sitting here expecting that some liberal Democrat is going to deliver us from all of this, and why don't we get busy?"

And so I became an advocate of the philosophy of self-help, and I'm still an advocate of that philosophy. I still support Booker T. Washington's posture ... but I wouldn't be doing my job here if I didn't raise some questions, with all due respect, about the relevancy of that philosophy and of this activity to a contemporary scene. I am dubious about the relevance.

Forty years after the Civil Rights Act and the Voting Rights Act, two generations after the glory days, 7 percent of adult black men are under lock and key today. One out of 14 adult African-American males in the country is in an institution somewhere. Meanwhile, there is a four-year gap in the intellectual development of African-American 17-year-olds as compared to whites, as measured by the U.S. Department of Education's systematic review of educational progress. The median income of African-American families relative to white families in the United States has barely budged from the mid-1970s. There's a big black middle class, which represents a lot of progress, but some 30 percent of black children are living in poverty.

Meanwhile, 30 million immigrants have come to the country since the liberalization of immigration laws in the 1960s, mostly from Asia and from Latin America. And guess what? The American dream is working for these people, by and large. What the immigrants say is, we may be illegal, but we're working our tails off. Sadly, those of us who would want to make a brief for African-Americans in depressed urban neighborhoods can't make the same argument. We can't claim that we are a contributing population, we are doing the best we can under difficult circumstances, we are working our tails off, you need us, you couldn't get by without us, but we're catching hell and you ought to give us a hand. We can't make the same argument the immigrants can.

We are still trading on a legacy that is two and three generations old, still invoking the moral authority of a long-forgotten, practically forgotten time, still talking about lynchings and Jim Crow.

Need for New Attitude

Now, the question I want to raise is whether it makes sense for us to celebrate bygone glory, evoke the philosophy of long-dead leaders, and express romantic rhetoric of African-Americans as a distinct people. Are we really a people? I don't mean to be unduly provocative, but I have a serious question in mind. Do we have the discipline, do we have the institutional capacity, do we have the vision, do we have the leadership, to be able to act in concert, to be able to define collective goals and aspirations and then to solve through collective action the problems that impede those goals and aspirations? That's what a "people" do, a "people" who have a language and culture, who have a narrative of collective aspiration, who have the institutions to enable them to govern themselves, and who can have goals and strive toward them.

The question is, are we African-Americans in the twenty-first century, a people? Thirty-five million strong, spread across a continent, with all manner of diverse interests – are we a people? Can we educate our children? Can we elaborate a philosophy of self-understanding, of identity, and of collective aspiration? And then can we pass it on to our children? It's a simple question. Do we have the capacity and the will to educate our children after our fashion? I fear that the answer must be no.

Bill Cosby stood up at Spelman College and told the women assembled there to graduate that they had better get busy because there aren't any good black men out there. All the men are in jail. All the men are messed up. Interestingly, Cosby stopped short of the obvious implication, which is that these women should marry white men.

Why not tell the graduates of Spelman College to find the best husband you can regardless of his color? Might it not be the best advice that one could give to an African-American woman today – to forget about the romantic notion of an African-American "people" and simply go out for herself and do the best she can as an individual? I don't think that the answer to that question is obvious at all.

Need for Inclusion

The major barrier to the fulfillment of the promise of American democracy for black Americans is the incompleteness of the incorporation of the descendants of slaves into the body politic, and that's a problem for the country. Our democracy's not complete. We have a problem here.

But is it a problem that can be solved by the rhetoric and the imagery of peoplehood for African-Americans? By the evocation of long-past leaders? By talking in terms of some kind of essentiality of a black community legacy which we only need to "get back to," if only we could get back to it, if only we could recover the lost virtues?

I believe this kind of rhetoric is outmoded and is not relevant to the problem of black Americans' incomplete incorporation into the American body politic. The only relevant "people" in this conversation about the condition of African-Americans is the American people.

This point is fundamental for me. The conversation about what blacks must do and what Americans must do has been interlaced for more than a century. When Booker T. Washington stood at that Atlanta Exposition in 1895 and gave that great speech, he was talking to blacks, Southern whites, and Northern whites, engaging in a very multidimensional and very complex, multilayered kind of public discourse where there were multiple audiences to whom varied messages needed to be sent. And so it has been all down through the years.

There are two different levels of conversation here. One is about what we, African-Americans, should do; and the other is about what we, Americans, should do. And they've often gotten confused.

The observation that African-Americans must take responsibility for our condition is an existential claim: You can't be a people if you can't educate your children. End of statement. It's not a claim about political ideology, it's not a claim about the shape of the welfare state, and it's not a statement about how big the tax rate should be, whether or not there should be a capital gains tax or free health care to anybody who wants it. It's a statement about what it means to carry yourself with your head high in the wake of your ancestors having been slaves.

Need for Community

In 1895 in Atlanta, Booker T. Washington stood closer to the institution of slavery than I stand right now to Martin Luther King, and the problem he was dealing with was an existential problem: If you want to be citizens, make yourselves fit to be citizens, he said. You say there's somebody out there who hates you? Well, this is the real world. There's somebody out there who hates you. But guess what? There are many opportunities at hand. Get busy dealing with them.

That was an existential argument to African-Americans. We could still make that argument today. But Washington was arguing to a population that was geographically concentrated in the south of the United States; that was culturally homogenous; that had institutions because of the requirements and the necessity of their separation. They were segregated. It was a necessity to create institutions. Of course they educated their own children. Who else would do it?

What we speak about now are cities with hundreds of thousands of people mired in a dead end. It is not a community. It does not have an articulated social structure of middle-class and upper-class people and educated workers and carpenters and all the rest living together in harmony. The civil society, mediating institutions are thin. Don't get me wrong: I'm for them. Let's build some more of them.

But I'm trying to be realistic: How are these kids going to get educated? That is an American problem, a public problem for this country. There aren't any shortcuts or easy answers to it. There's not going to be a cultural fix to this problem. You're not going to talk a million black men out of prison. There are structural problems here, and it's not all the government's fault. If we want a strategy to deal with this problem, it must be a public strategy; it must be an American strategy. We'll have to deal with the laws and institutions that influence our people, and we have to talk about it as an American community.

Need for Common Agenda

So, the point of dissent – if it is a point of dissent – that I wish to state here, is that while I am inspired by the example of Booker T. Washington and have great reverence and respect for it and for the labors of my friend and colleague Lee Walker over these decades in promoting and advancing it, the one thing I don't think is going to solve the problem is black parents suddenly taking more responsibility for their children (although of course that is a good thing in itself).

Our country has a serious problem. The solution might cost us some tax money. It might mean that we have to think in a radically different way about how we organize our various activities. It might mean a lot of things. But let us not think that we can fix it all just by exhorting the black community to get its act together, reorient themselves, and bring back Booker T. Washington's philosophy.

Saying that things will get better if we bring back Washington's philosophy and try to make self-help take root in the black community is a phony argument. Cook County Jail doesn't have enough cells. You can't drive your car after midnight in no-go zones in this city. There are kids who basically don't have a chance from the time they're five years old. It's a public problem and an American problem, and American institutions are going to have to deal with it.

That will require the help, support, and enthusiastic engagement of civil society within the black community, but looking at the scale of the problem, looking at the history that has brought us here, and being realistic about it, it seems to me that we can't avoid the conclusion that the people we need to mobilize, the people to whom we must appeal, are the American people, not some romantic, historical invocation of an African-American peoplehood that might have been relevant 50 years ago, and certainly was relevant 100 years ago, but is no longer relevant today.

Chapter 3

Sowing, Reaping, Owning

Rev. William "Bill" Winson[5]

It's a pleasure to speak on behalf of the legacy that was left by Booker T. Washington. I have a special appreciation for Washington's legacy, because I was brought up in the shadow of Tuskegee.

I'm going to talk about the legacy of Booker T. Washington, which made a mark in my life – so much so, that as I describe some of the things that are happening in my life now, you'll see that it's almost duplicating that legacy.

I was born in Tuskegee, Alabama. My dad would take me on Sundays after church to Moton Field where the Tuskegee Airmen trained. At that time it was a full gamut of fighter pilots and airplanes, and it was a huge operation. The employee count in the military at Tuskegee at that time was about 15,000. As I grew up, I got role models impressed in my heart just by going there and seeing it.

And there was another industry in Tuskegee other than aviation. It was the medical industry. The fifth-largest VA hospital in the world was at Tuskegee. At that time, many black physicians could not do their residencies and so forth at any other locations except those which served the African-American community. So the colleges sent their doctors to Tuskegee to do their residency and internship. That was the second industry.

The third industry was education. There was the Tuskegee Institute, which is now Tuskegee University.

'Lifting the Veil of Ignorance'

Those three institutions made an impression on my life. They caused me to gain a real idea of what leadership is. And right in the middle of the campus there at Tuskegee, there is this monument – a person who had been a slave,

---

[5] Rev. William "Bill" S. Winston is founder and pastor of Living Word Christian Center, a 15,000-member church located in Forest Park, Illinois.

partially dressed, and another person standing over him pulling up a veil. And the caption reads, "Lifting the veil of ignorance."

That was the legacy of Booker T. Washington, to lift the veil of ignorance in people's lives. He wanted to improve the way people lived in the Deep South, especially the "colored people" at that time. There were masses of poverty in the South, and he was out to change that.

He also wanted to lift the veil of ignorance off the Negro race and bring people into a place where they could compete in society. He also wanted to shift a paradigm – he wanted to attack the very source of attitudes in the South at that time. He was a man of vision. Vision is seeing something that may occur in the future, it's a snapshot of somebody's future or a clear picture of conditions that do not currently exist. A vision could be a mental picture of somebody's destiny, or it could be the ability to see opportunities that other people don't see in their current circumstances.

Washington was a visionary, but he was also a leader. A leader is one who guides by influence, one whom others want to follow, one who leads others to leadership, one who possesses both character and competence. He was a leader.

So Booker T. Washington was a visionary leader. He could see something that did not currently exist. He could see opportunities in circumstances that were devastating. His book *Up from Slavery* should be required reading for everyone who goes through any kind of college or university. In that book, he describes his beginning and his challenges and his ending. He said, "Political agitation alone would not save the Negro. Back of the ballot he must have property, industry, skill, economy, intelligence, and character." He's saying that without these, blacks would not permanently succeed.

Calling for Economic Improvement

Booker T. Washington was in favor of social action, but the thing that I picked up from him was his call for economic action. He really was a catalyst in terms of driving black economic development. He said, "The whole future of the Negro rested largely upon the question as to whether or not he should make himself, through skill, intelligence, and character, of such undeniable value to the community in which he lived that the community could not dispense with his presence." That's what he was after, and he was remarkably successful.

A measure of Booker T. Washington's success appeared in a book from an organization called Business Reform, an organization that put out a Christian business magazine called *Christian Business Reform*. I read the book about leaders such as Henry Ford and Booker T. Washington, and I read something about Washington that I had never seen before. It said this: "In 1905 Booker T. Washington and Tuskegee turned out more self-made millionaires than Harvard, Yale, and Princeton combined." That was a startling statement to me.

Now, what did he do? He introduced into society people with skills that were indispensable. And he trained them to such a level, with excellence and character, that the society at large could not do without them.

In one of his graduating classes, they went out and they began to farm and produced 250 bushels of sweet potatoes per acre. The white farmers surrounding this farm produced 49 bushels per acre. They began to come over to the black farmers to find out what they were doing.

Now what am I getting at? Booker T. Washington said, "Any individual who learned to do something better than anybody else, learned to do a common thing in an uncommon manner, has solved his problems, regardless of the color of his skin, and the proportion as the Negro learned to produce what other people wanted and must have, in the same proportion would he be respected."

Contributing to Society

It's kind of interesting how people try to garner respect – and of course we should respect everybody – but they have made no contribution. Booker T. Washington was going to make it so that the Negro would have such a contribution that he could not be denied respect. He realized that economics drove a lot of society. He realized that, of course, as he was trying to raise money for the school. As you know, he started with a church and a little shanty. Sometimes when he ate breakfast, they held an umbrella over his head when it was raining because the roof was leaking.

I read all of that. I had gone and visited the Carver museum many times. Why? Because the visions of leaders determine the influence they have on other people. And so Washington drew people like George Washington Carver. Carver produced more than 300 products out of the peanut. Face cream, crayons, you name it. He said he went and asked God, what is the peanut made for? God said, what do you want to know about it? Carver said, can I get milk out of a peanut? Carver said God said to him, what kind of milk do you want? Jersey milk, Borden House milk? What kind of milk? And God told him how to take the peanut apart and put it back together again.

Carver said no books ever went into his laboratory. He called it God's little workshop. He said he goes in, and once he goes in, God pulls back the curtain. You see, there's another level that we can operate in. I think sometimes we get so academic that we forget: We are made after God's own image and in his likeness.

Realizing a Vision

I have learned a lot from Booker T. Washington. I have learned how to persevere, because I read about him persevering, and heard it many times.

When I was in elementary school, it was at a school called Chambliss Children's House. It was an experimental school started by Tuskegee Institute. In the third grade we were speaking French. They trained us so that we would score much above average on any of the national merit examinations. And they were training us to be leaders. We saw people such as the leaders of Liberia – they wouldn't come to Tuskegee without coming to our school and talking to us. This type of leadership is what he put into the students.

And there was more. At that school I saw a horse bow down, and that was Roy Rogers' horse. He brought him because the veterinary medicine school at Tuskegee was, and is still, the premiere vet med school in the world. Washington built it and drew talented people. This is what came out of Tuskegee. And it can come out of any place with a person carrying a vision like the one that was carried by Booker T. Washington.

As I look at Booker T. Washington's own life, I look at the economic side of it and how he affected me. My wife and I went into the ministry. She came from IBM, in the technical side of things, programming large computers. I finished Tuskegee in pre-med but decided I wanted to go into the military. I flew fighter airplanes for years, and then I joined IBM and rose in that company. My wife and I left in 1985 and went into the full-time ministry.

We went to seminary and came back to Chicago with no money, only $200 to my name. A dear sister took us in – that reminds me of Booker T. Washington, because he stayed with some families when he first went to Tuskegee. And when he stayed with those families, he said oftentimes they would set the table but they would have only one fork, and they'd give him that one fork and let him eat with it.

I started services in a little storefront church. I didn't know it until it rained, but the roof leaked. And when I came to have services on Sunday, the floor was full of water, and I'd have to mop everything up before everybody came. But I persevered, and the reason I did is because I had a vision. Just like him. He slept on the floor in many places, he said. He said sometimes they had a floor covering, and there was wood on the floor, but sometimes they had nothing, and he slept on the ground itself. But he slept on it.

Sowing and Reaping

Washington believed in sowing and reaping – I have some of the sermons that he taught in the chapel. Some of the biggest things he taught were character and integrity. What do you do when nobody's looking?

He taught people how to stay the course. It's impossible for you to enter into the Promised Land without integrity. Even though your job may not be the premier job that you would like to have, if you serve whoever you're working for in the highest regard, you'll reap a harvest. And he constantly showed them how to do that and talked to them about it.

What he talked about is ownership. He was moving people into ownership because he knew that ownership was the true path to wealth. Sometimes people are trying to create wealth with a job, and it's very hard to do that.

One of the challenges that he had one time was making bricks. He didn't know anything about bricklaying. In Tuskegee right now they still have a section of Tuskegee called Brickyard Hill. That's where they made bricks. Now, what was he making bricks for? He was making bricks because he was going to build a university. Nobody was giving him money. So he finally borrowed $200 from General Armstrong, a mentor of Booker T. Washington from Hampton University. He had no money to buy the bricks, so he set out to make the bricks.

A very wealthy lady who apparently owned some kind of brick foundry heard about it in Tuskegee. Her husband had died, and she told Washington he could use the foundry. So he took the students there to make bricks. He said it was hard work. They made something like 25,000 or 35,000 bricks. But the bricks were not made right, and when pressure was put on them they crumbled. He had borrowed $200, had tried it three times and the bricks had failed each time, and he was up against the odds again. What did he do? He persisted. He took his gold watch, which had been given to him by a very wealthy lady in Boston, and although he wanted to save it, he pawned that gold watch. He got $25 or $30 for it.

He came back and made the last effort on making those bricks. This time, the bricks held. That was called the story of "bricks without straw" – the reference to straw means having no money to make the bricks.

Building Skill

All of this helps us gain a respect for Washington and how he worked to build skill in the people. He wanted to build respect for the black community. He wanted to do it through our own efforts – he didn't believe in entitlements and people begging for things. He wanted people to have respect for themselves and for others to have respect for them.

That helped me, because as we began to grow here in Chicago, God began to enlarge my vision and began to tell me what he wanted from me. So I enlarged our reach into the business arena. Today we have about 15,000 members. We have a school called the Joseph Business School – it's the only Christian business school of its kind in the nation. It's certified by the State of Illinois and is a regional headquarters for the Small Business Administration. We have instructors – some from Wharton, some from Harvard, some from the University of Chicago and Northwestern – and these people are teaching other people from our inner cities how to run and operate their own businesses, producing entrepreneurs.

What we're doing is lifting the veil of ignorance. We're taking people from just existing in this city to being able to make a true living for themselves.

Consider some numbers. Twenty percent of African-Americans today have no health insurance. Today 1.4 million black men – 13 percent of the race – have lost the right to vote because of felony convictions. Eight million blacks live in poverty. Blacks are on the bottom of every economic scale.

By 2009, the good news is that the buying power of black people is expected to be about $965 billion. And we have to watch for what Farrah Gray, an African-American who became a millionaire at 14 years old, observed recently: "People own Land Cruisers, Land Rovers, and still have landlords." That's not the idea. The idea is that we own.

I looked up the figures on business revenue for 2002 in Chicago: roughly $144 billion. How much of that is from the black community? 1.2 percent. Why? Blacks make up almost 40 percent of the population in Chicago, yet 1.2 percent of business revenue is going to the black community. What's wrong with that number? They don't own anything.

What was Booker T. Washington after? What is Bill Winston after? Creating ownership. Creating people who have some economic say in what's going on here today. And through ownership, people can rise in respect and in influence.

PART 2

THE MAN AND THE LEGACY

Chapter 4

A Problem of Respectability

Glenn C. Loury, Ph.D.[6]

I want to underscore one aspect of something that Rev. Winston said. I think that Rev. Winston's recollection about the work of Booker T. Washington and the problem of respectability is something that really deserves to be emphasized, because we African-Americans still have a problem of respectability.

There's a deep truth in Booker T. Washington's legacy about how one must manage that problem. It is that insisting on respect from others, demanding it, in the name of justice, in the name of what is right, saying we ought to be respected – and of course, everyone ought to be respected – ultimately is not a satisfactory strategy. Respectability is not something that you can demand from people. It's something that has to be earned on the basis of what you do with your life.

The circumstances in which African-Americans exist today in the United States are of course very different from those that faced Booker T. Washington a few decades after the end of slavery. But the problem of respectability is still with us. The problem is generated by the vast over-representation of African-Americans among those who are suffering from all the various maladies of dysfunction and marginality in society. The prisons are very black in this country – that can't not be noticed. You can't ask people to not notice that.

---

[6] Dr. Glenn C. Loury is the Merton P. Stoltz Professor of Social Sciences in the economics department of Brown University.

The disparity in educational achievement, especially at the top, is stark and glaring. You go to the places at the very cutting edge of science and technology in this country – such as Cal Tech, MIT, Stanford, and Princeton – and you will find people from every corner of the globe, including Africa, but you will find very few African-Americans at these places. Our middle class in this era of freedom over the past 30 years has not produced what we ought to have produced in terms of excellence and outstanding achievement at the very top of the most competitive fields. There are reasons. We can give the reasons why. It's not that this can't be explained; this is not a reflection of an inherent inadequacy of African-Americans.

Image Problem

But nevertheless, this circumstance creates a problem of image. There is a problem of perception in the minds of others that has to be dealt with. In my humble opinion, one thing that we get from the legacy of Booker T. Washington is an acknowledgment of that problem and then an acceptance of the burden and the responsibility to face it directly. And facing it directly means we have to act in ways that engender a positive response from others, not simply insist upon them, because what you get out of that is patronization. You get a kind of, "Oh, sure, yes, we understand, we'll give you respect. Oh yes, oh sure, you do deserve a place at the table. Absolutely, 10 percent of the positions, no doubt about it."

But underneath that is contempt. Contempt for our weakness, contempt for the fact that we don't actually do the things we need to be doing to earn respectability. I'm not saying there's something wrong with black folks that we can't fix. This is something we can fix. I'm saying, however, that we have to recognize the need to fix it. We have to recognize that this problem of respectability can't really be faced in any way other than by actions on our part that earn the respect of others.

Chapter 5

The Legacy of Tuskegee

Robert J. Norell, Ph.D.[7]

It is a great pleasure to talk about Booker Washington. I have long been engaged with the history of Tuskegee. I wrote a doctoral dissertation about the Civil Rights movement in Tuskegee. I'm a native of Alabama. I spent my whole life there until I went to college. Yet during those years I never went to Tuskegee, which I think is a testament to segregation in Alabama in the 1950s and 1960s. But I got much engaged with civil rights and then was by accident led to focus on Tuskegee as a community study of the roots of the Civil Rights movement in local communities and local institutions.

For a long period of time I worked on an overview, kind of a synthetic treatment of the big picture of American race relations, wherein I really started to try to offer a revisionist understanding of Booker Washington. To borrow a phrase, I tried to "lift the veil of ignorance" about Booker Washington from the liberal academic community in which I had been trained. After doing work in Tuskegee and thinking about it for 25 years, I have come to believe that the academic community's interpretations and understandings of Washington are really quite wrong.

Rev. Winston alluded to it when he said there's two schools of thought about Booker T. Washington. One is that he offers a role model for economic and educational development that all Americans should follow, especially African-Americans. The other view says he was a sell-out, an Uncle Tom. That is the view that overwhelmingly prevails in the academy. But it is one that I have departed from in the course of doing a great deal of research on Tuskegee, the environment there, and on Booker Washington the person.

---

[7] Dr. Robert J. Norell is professor of history and holds the Bernadotte Schmitt Chair of Excellence at the University of Tennessee.

Washington's Changing Reputation

I understand there are many people here who have a quite positive understanding of Booker T. Washington, but I think it's important to understand that is not shared in the academy and to a large extent in the popular mind. Washington has been viewed as a symbol of the age in which he lived. Washington understood his symbolic role and acted always to shape its meaning, but I think he often failed to persuade his audience of the object lessons he meant to teach.

In *The Souls of Black Folk* in 1903, W.E.B. DuBois asserted that Washington's program practically accepts the inferiority of the Negro races. In Washington's 1895 Atlanta Exposition speech, which DuBois derided as "the Atlanta Compromise," a pejorative description that has endured, Washington accepted the denial of black citizenship rights, according to DuBois.

Washington, DuBois admitted, was striving nobly to make Negro artisans, businessmen, and property owners. But DuBois argued that it is utterly impossible for the working man and property owners to defend their rights and succeed without the right of suffrage, which DuBois suggested Washington had willingly and happily given up on behalf of other African-Americans.

I think DuBois's argument is entirely erroneous. In the years after Washington's death in 1915, little was added to DuBois's critique – and in fact in the first generation after his death, historical writing about Washington was really quite positive. Carter Woodson, Emmett J. Scott, Horace Mann Bond, Charles Spurgeon Johnson – all had very positive views of Washington. So did James Weldon Johnson, and this attitude toward Washington carried through into the 1930s.

But in the 1940s, we began to see a turn led by scholars, largely under the influence of the radical politics of the 1930s, who began to compare Washington unfavorably to DuBois, whose radical politics, of course, were much more to the liking of left-wing scholars. A younger generation of black historians, and some white historians, began to offer a much more critical view of Washington.

The most notable one was C. Vann Woodward's 1951 *Origins of the New South*, which portrayed Washington as essentially a dupe of wealthy businessmen and white conservatives in the South and essentially a person who had acquiesced in segregation and all the awful race relations that had become entrenched in the South around the turn of the twentieth century.

Rise of DuBois

It is important to understand, though, that the crucial time of interpretation that influences us today came in the 1960s with the Civil Rights movement. And there, Washington was a convenient opposite to place against the protest orientation that African-Americans embraced in that decade as part of the Civil Rights movement.

The elevation of DuBois as the model for African-American protest, as sort of the father of protest, then became the popular one that activists and then historians and sociologists embraced. The other side of that coin was that Booker Washington had to be demonized as a sell-out, as an Uncle Tom.

It's really remarkable to see the ways that the DuBoisian interpretation of Washington is almost entirely adopted by scholars. Essentially, whatever DuBois said about Washington is embraced, first by Vann Woodward, and then by his student Louis Harlan, and then by subsequent scholars. By now almost two generations of scholars writing about American race relations have essentially followed what DuBois said and adopted his very biased view of Washington. It's really remarkable. I'm not aware of any other circumstance in which one person who is the avowed enemy of another historical figure gets to essentially establish what the historical reputation of the other person is.

The crucial person in developing this interpretation, after Vann Woodward, was Louis Harlan, who wrote a two-volume biography of Washington, the first volume published in 1972, the second in 1983, and was the editor of some 15 volumes of Booker Washington's papers.

Harlan was a very talented historian and a fine writer who has an amazing hostility to Booker T. Washington. One wonders why a person who is so negative and so hostile toward a historical figure would choose to write a biography about him. Louis Harlan will tell you that he began his study in the 1960s with the assumption that Washington was an Uncle Tom, that he was a sell-out, and then he worked on research and writing about Washington for the next 25 years. He has said that along the way he became more respectful of Washington because he wasn't purely a sell-out, just a sneaky, underhanded man.

Harlan's opinion was very much shaped by the fact that he was working at the Library of Congress between 1969 and the early 1980s, and as a very good liberal Harlan began to see a historical analogy to Booker Washington in Richard Nixon. He saw Washington as a sneaky, evil person, an evil genius. That is essentially the interpretation he offers. Harlan won the Pulitzer Prize and two major book awards for historians, and his much-celebrated book has essentially shaped the writing and understanding of Booker Washington ever since.

Willful Misinterpretation

I think there are some real problems with this approach, obviously. In my work, I essentially have said three or four things in response to this approach, and I will briefly touch on them now.

First, the writing on Washington by scholars, at least in the modern period, from the Civil Rights movement forward, has not placed him accurately in the context of Tuskegee and of the white South where he had to work. The hostility to black education – and I mean any black education, not just classical education or liberal education – the hostility toward even industrial education from whites in the South in the 1890s and the first two decades of the twentieth century was vicious and virulent.

Men such as Ben Tillman in South Carolina, Tom Heflin in Alabama, James K. Vardaman in Mississippi, and the novelist Thomas Dixon argued that Washington's commitment to black education was ultimately a challenge to white supremacy These were intensely racist political leaders who were open in their intense hostility to Washington and far more popular than some of the more liberal-minded whites, a few of whom were Washington's friends. These racist leaders said that if enough black people were educated, they would do well in society and rise and challenge the Jim Crow system.

Hence it's very important to understand that Washington was working in an intensely hostile environment. Tuskegee was a very tense place. A lot of white people in that community were very nervous about the very existence of the institute and of Washington's aggressive growth of the institute. Washington had to be very careful in how he behaved and what he said.

It's important to understand that, with all of that, he still continued to speak out. He has not been given credit in the historical record for the many strong statements he made about lynching, about disfranchisement, about all of the atrocities of the Jim Crow system. What scholars have focused on are the more ambiguous statements he made in large public places.

Thus Washington has been extricated from the real and accurate context in which he had to work, and as a result he has been placed almost entirely in the context of a conflict with DuBois. In fact, Harlan does not recognize fully, as he should, the intensely personal nature of the conflict between DuBois and Washington. These two men just didn't like each other, and they vied for the leadership of the race and for recognition from influential white Americans about what to do about African-Americans in this society. Booker Washington almost always won those discussions and debates and contests at the time, and DuBois was intensely hostile to him and did all kinds of personal things. And to be sure, Washington did a lot of rather personal backbiting in return.

Working Within Limits

But in the end, what has happened is that all of the evidence for shaping the historical reputation has been loaded on the negative side of Booker Washington. It's very important that we get beyond the historical interpretation that suggests that the only way the African-American group can rise in America is through aggressive street protest, which is essentially the message of academic treatises and writings since the 1960s. Such an understanding is essential if we are to achieve not just a truthful, more accurate understanding of Washington but also a more balanced understanding of the possibilities and needs of group leadership, ethnic or racial leadership in American society, of what is potentially successful and what is not.

It seems to me one of the things that scholars have assumed is that black leaders have to be in the model of Frederick Douglass or Martin King: They have to be lions, they can't ever be foxes, they can never effectively be subtle and indirect.

Booker T. Washington was a man way ahead of his time in how he understood communications and the way Americans came to believe what they believe. Much of that he shaped by indirect means as he lived in a viciously racist time. In my view he did what he could, within the limits of human capacity.

Chapter 6

Tuskegee Principles for the Information Age

Marcus D. Pohlmann, Ph.D.[8]

I'm going to be drawing on my teaching of Booker Washington for more than 20 years and on some research that I've been doing recently on the Memphis City Schools.

Washington spoke and wrote at a time of serious economic crisis in the African-American community. He looked around and concluded that with the right type of education, blacks could develop themselves into economic commodities that, in the turn of the century marketplace, would be employable. In his Atlanta Exposition address Washington stated, "Our greatest danger is that we may overlook the fact that the masses of us are to live by the productions of our hands, and to fail to keep in mind that we shall prosper in proportion as we learn to dignify and glorify common labor and put brains and skills into the common occupations of life, shall prosper in proportion as we learn to draw the line between the superficial and the substantial."

To that end he founded Tuskegee Institute in large part to build the kind of character, ambition, and manual skills the market seemed to demand – a good fit for the largely agricultural South and the emerging industrial cities of the North and eventually of the South. There were in fact many opportunities emerging for those with basic skills, a solid work ethic, and the ability to distinguish between, as Washington put it, "the superficial and the substantial." If Washington was alive today he might well be just as concerned about some of the realities that we observe in the twenty-first century African-American community.

Serious Problems

It is an all-too-familiar litany. The high school dropout rate for black males is more than 50 percent in many large cities. The black adult illiteracy rate

---

[8] Dr. Marcus D. Pohlmann is a professor and chairman of the Political Science Department at Rhodes College.

is nearly three times that of white adults. More than 40 percent of all black teenagers have problems, serious problems, in terms of literacy. Only 13 percent of black men ages 25 and older hold a B.A. degree. There are more blacks in prison than in college.

Not surprisingly, given these facts, blacks and whites remain far apart economically. Blacks remain twice as likely to be unemployed or among the working poor, and three times as likely to live below the poverty level and in overcrowded housing.

In addition, the majority of black children are now raised by a single mother, and three out of four of those children will experience some form of poverty by the age of 11. The median net worth of the average African-American family is 10 times lower than that of whites, roughly half owning assets worth $5,000 or less, nearly a third with nearly no assets or in debt, and only 10 percent of black households with any stock or mutual funds.

Although serious problems clearly continue, today's economic circumstances are considerably different from the ones Booker T. Washington faced in the nation's industrializing period. A century after he wrote, as the twenty-first century dawns, we find ourselves in a postindustrial economy. The mechanization and mobility of industries have cost many lesser-skilled city workers the opportunity to hold promising, unionized factory jobs.

Meanwhile, an ever-increasing proportion of available American jobs can be found in the professional and personal services. These tend to be in fields such as health care, finance, insurance, retail sales, and government. More Americans are now employed by Wal-Mart and McDonald's than by General Motors and U.S. Steel.

A number of well-paid skilled positions remain in this nation's more service-oriented economy. The list includes positions such as physical therapists, store managers, and litigators. Such work involves specialized training, knowledge, and what economists call being "geographically situated." These jobs tend to generate the kind of wages, benefits, skill development, and opportunities for advancement that place the workers in what is called the primary labor market. They afford the kind of comfort and security normally associated with middle-class status, and if enough wealth can be accumulated they can even elevate one into the owning class.

Low-Wage Positions

Far more of today's new postindustrial positions, however, now fall under what has been called the secondary labor market. These are jobs with little prospect of launching one into the more secure middle-class. They tend to be lesser-skilled jobs in restaurants, retail stores, and private hospitals. Forty percent of our current jobs can be learned in less than a month and are generally low-paying. They often pay little more than minimum wage and entail few if any benefits such as health insurance, paid vacations, paid holidays, or a retirement plan. They involve little or no skill development or opportunities for significant advancement, and many are part-time.

One-quarter of the current U.S. workforce now earns wages that would leave them below the federal poverty level even after a 40-hour work week. In 2004, some 37 million Americans found themselves below the federal government's poverty line, and 57 million more would be classified as near-poor, meaning their incomes are below poverty or within two times the poverty level. One in four working Americans can now be classified as poor or near poor.

Thus the postindustrial economy has tended to create jobs at the top and at the bottom of the employment ladder, with those in the top brackets requiring more skills and more education than ever before. Meanwhile, there are fewer established, stable bottom rungs from which underskilled workers can successfully begin their way up the ladder of economic success. This does not bode well for the urban poor trying to rise out of the inner cities of the twentieth century.

As Douglas Massey put it, "in a globalized economy, two classes can be expected to fare well and one poorly. Owners of financial and human capital, the wealthy and the educated, will do well because the things they offer on the global market – money, knowledge, and skills – are in short supply. Owners of labor – workers – will not do well because what they offer – physical work effort – is cheap, plentiful, and over-supplied on a global scale."

Stanford University economics professor Martin Carnoy has found that the middle-class workers who managed to ride the top of the postindustrial technological wave have tended to be those with educations that allowed them to process and analyze information. Meanwhile, those with manual skills or few skills at all tended to miss that technological wave and sink into the service sector's sea of secondary labor market opportunities.

Nevertheless, in a relatively recent Gallup poll, taken almost a century after Booker T. Washington wrote, the Horatio Alger myth seems to be alive and well. Nearly two-thirds of the adults over 30 years of age consider themselves at least somewhat likely to be rich in their lifetimes. One of the primary bulwarks of that faith is the belief that education provides a vehicle for anyone to rise almost limitlessly if the person is talented enough, has enough ambition, and works hard. Besides training the nation's workforce, universal public education was to level the playing field, so that all children would have a relatively equal opportunity to develop their talents and succeed in America's free-market system.

Abysmal Education

So how are the Horatio Algers, ragged Dicks, and tattered Toms actually doing in the new millennium? Real people residing in large United States cities such as Chicago will almost certainly begin their ascent in an urban public school. What do they find?

First, it should be noted that there is clear empirical evidence that schooling helps determine one's job, which in turn determines one's income and wealth. Each additional year of schooling up to a point adds an additional 10 percent to an individual's earnings. A college graduate makes an average of 59 percent more than a high school graduate, and more than three times that of a grade school graduate.

The same is even truer for wealth accumulation, where a college graduate has more than seven times the financial assets of a high school graduate and some 32 times that of a grade school graduate.

So who gets the higher levels of education? Here it gets more complicated. To begin with, students who do better in school are more likely to have the opportunity to advance, but higher achievement appears to be linked to one's family attributes. The more income and education one's parents have, the more likely their children will further their educations. Some of the most recent RAND data suggest that the gap in educational attainment between the children of haves and the children of have-nots has actually increased since the late 1970s.

When the impediments of race and poverty come together, we find scarcely more than 1 percent of African-American students from the poorest category of households attend college full-time. Not surprisingly, weak students from well-off families stand a better chance of attending college than better students coming from poorer backgrounds.

Overall, then, education can very significantly affect one's economic position in life, but the economic class into which one is born has a clear impact on one's education. One's ultimate socioeconomic position appears to be at least in part a function of the socioeconomic circumstances into which one was born. The socioeconomic circumstances into which most inner-city children are born do not bode well for a twenty-first century rags-to-riches metamorphosis in a city such as Memphis, Tennessee.

Memphis Case Study

My own current research involves analyzing contemporary educational opportunities, in particular in the city of Memphis. First of all, Memphis does indeed represent what has come to be called a postindustrial city. Virtually all of the city's large manufacturers are gone. The mechanization and mobility of industries have left most of the city's lesser-skilled workers in the service sector. Poverty is both extreme and intense. The *Metropolitan Area Fact Book* noted that Memphis had the second-poorest black population in the nation and the highest infant mortality rate of any of the nation's 60 largest cities. In 2005, one-fourth of the city lived below the federal government's poverty level.

Memphis City Schools is the largest school system in the state of Tennessee, and one of the largest in the country. It has 120,000 students and more than 190 school buildings, spending about a billion dollars a year. Demographically, the city schools are roughly 90 percent minority. Three in four of those students qualify for federally subsidized school meals, meaning they are poor or near poor. One in four students in Memphis transfers in or out of school over the course of the year as they move from residence to residence. In some of the schools defined as failing under current federal mandates, the turnover in the course of the school year is as high as 70 percent.

How are these students faring academically in the postindustrial period when formal education has become so incredibly essential? Taken together, the combination of standard tests and value-added scores describe a student body that starts disproportionately low and tends to fall farther behind as the years go by. In the end, the graduation rate in the Memphis City Schools is only 60 percent, and it has been declining.

Unprepared Students

At Cherokee Elementary School in Memphis, for example, one-fourth of the students will transfer in or out over the course of the normal school year. Roughly 85 percent of them live in poverty. There's no active PTA. It's not unusual for one or two parents out of 20 to turn out for a parent-teacher conference in any of the given grades. Students often arrive unbathed, inadequately clothed, and without all their books.

Leandre's story is not unlike those of many of his classmates at Cherokee Elementary. His mother is serving time for voluntary manslaughter, and his father was just released from prison but has yet to visit him. Leandre lives with his 20-year-old aunt Tarsha, who stays home with her one-year-old son and is on public assistance.

Or consider some examples from some preschools in the Memphis area. There's Tweetie, who came to school not even knowing his first or last name. There's Jasper, who teachers took three months to understand anything that he was saying. There's Malika, whose standard response to greetings for the first month she was at school was pretty much limited to "Shut up."

"It's heartbreaking," says Patricia Reeves, who has been teaching kindergarten for the past 28 years. "Some of the children can't even count to five, they don't know their colors, they can't concentrate, often they don't know how to interact with other children."

Neglected Children

There is an emerging body of scientific evidence suggesting how critical the first five years are in shaping a child's capacity to learn. It appears to be very essential to brain development that they be spoken to, read to, cuddled, and allowed to engage in physical play. There are what the scientists call short, critical periods when those parts of the brain that control vision and language are open to be stimulated. There are also what they call sensitive periods that shape a child's ability to learn math, music, and second languages. Brain scans verify these findings, and they are further supported by evidence of higher IQ scores that appear to last throughout the child's school years.

Dr. Jane Wiechel, president of the National Association for the Education of Young Children, concludes, "If you aren't exposed early in life to experiences that will enhance brain development, it is an unfortunate fact for your life that your brain's plasticity declines throughout the rest of it."

Poor children are talked to less and end up with vocabularies that are about half those of middle-class children. More than a decade ago an official at the Education Testing Service warned that five variables explain 90 percent of the achievement score differences between schools. The five variables were as follows: days absent, number of hours spent watching television, number of pages a student reported reading for homework, the extent and nature of the reading materials found in the home, and the number of parents in the home.

The federal government's Title I program puts its focus on providing remedial reading assistance, especially in the early elementary grades. David Sojourner, a friend of mine and long-time director of student information at Memphis City Schools, found Title I early childhood programs to be one of the few government initiatives that he has seen to post significant results. According to Sojourner, testing in the 1970s regularly showed inner-city children to be 18 to 24 months lower academically than their chronological age. After a year of Title I remediation, most of those children gained 12 months or more of mental age.

Effective Remediation

The Tennessee Perry School Project report, which some of you may be familiar with, studied children from their preschool experience until they turned 19 years of age. More of the preschool children ended up finishing high school, getting advanced education, being gainfully employed, and were less likely to become pregnant or get arrested. Preschool was seen as capable of reinforcing family support for education and a sense of personal responsibility, but not overcoming a negative orientation. It was also viewed as capable of helping students remain in school until non-family role models became more influential by adolescence. It was seen as building the kind of confidence that contributes to goal orientation.

When comparing Memphis-area children with and without preschool training, TCAP achievement test scores for first graders with preschool training average seven points higher across the board, and 12 points higher in the language exam. A particularly strong connection was noted between such training and a student's reading ability in the third grade.

There is additional empirical evidence that high-quality, intensive early education helps students come to school better prepared intellectually and socially. It appears to improve academic success, lower dropout rates, and reduce the need for special education programs and grade repetition. In the long term it can also increase the likelihood of subsequent education and training, and reduce delinquency risks, teen pregnancy, and welfare reliance. Such gains have been particularly noticeable in students from disadvantaged backgrounds.

Need for Tuskegee Approach

What I'm arguing is that we need information-age Tuskegee-like schools in every school district in every large city. They should be staffed by well-paid, highly trained, and motivated teachers. And they need to be optionally available from the age of one. I'm talking about K1, K2, K3, and K4 as optional, and mandatory K5 through grade 12.

We should also remember that from birth until age 18, today's average child will spend only about 9 percent of his or her time in school. Thus it is obvious that much of the educational process will inevitably have to occur in the home. Consequently, in addition to early intervention, finding ways to increase parental involvement has been a significant component of many of the comprehensive reform models utilized in school districts across the country.

Some have resulted in clear achievement score gains, especially among low-income minority students, but it is difficult to determine just how much of those gains is attributable to particular components of these programs. Nonetheless, Samuel Casey Carter notes that the common component of the 21 high-performing inner-city schools he studied was a parental contract, which required parents to read to their children, check homework, and monitor assignments.

At the earlier stages there are programs such as early Head Start, which began in 1996 with 143 programs. Early Head Start works with parents of infants from birth to age three. It teaches parents how to become better early educators of their infants. Early Head Start was a very important response to brain research, according to Helen Blank, director of child care for the Children's Defense Fund. Initial research results seem to bear this out, demonstrating that the beneficiaries of the program had better language, cognitive, and social skills than other three-year-olds.

Chicago's Cradle-to-the-Classroom program focuses on unwed teen mothers. Beginning prior to delivery, staff members arrange for access to prenatal care and make monthly home visits. After birth, the program sends trained mentors into the homes on a weekly basis. The mother is taught how to play cognitive learning games with her infant, beginning in the child's very first month. By age three, only 9 percent of the children were found to be at risk of developmental delays in language and social skills. The figure was 59 percent for a control group of babies with teen mothers who did not have the benefit of that program.

Big Investment

Nonetheless, enduring challenges remain. There is, for example, a growing body of empirical evidence that the value of early intervention begins to taper off as the child ages and other influences intervene, especially for inner-city children. There is also the fact that many of these children will bounce from relative to relative and there will simply not be a stable and consistent parent with whom to work. Consequently, poor children entering regular public schools may well need many of the same comprehensive services that are provided in programs such as Head Start – nutritionists, social workers, psychologists, and people employed to encourage parental involvement.

Of course, there is a large price tag. Tennessee is phasing in a statewide pre-kindergarten program that allows school districts to opt in gradually. It is to involve at least 5½ hours of instruction per day and will be staffed by certified teachers. This is a K4 program. The cost of making such education available for every four-year-old in the state is estimated to be roughly $170 million, or $100,000 for every 20-person classroom. If we want to extend that to K1, K2, and K3, you can do the mathematics.

If we are to be truly serious about leaving no child behind, in an age where formal education is far more essential than ever before, our nation's public schools must become the Tuskegee Institutes for the information age, from K1 through the 12th grade. And as a society we must be willing to spend the sizeable sum of money that will entail.

Chapter 7

Practical Assistance

Christopher R. Reed, Ph.D.[9]

I think I can say that if Booker T. Washington were alive today in Chicago (and he made many visits to Chicago), he would ask, "Professor Reed, what are you doing and what are your friends doing that's positive to solve problems that existed early in the twentieth century and problems that still might be around in the twenty-first century?"

And I would say, "Professor Washington, I was shown in the *Chicago Tribune* on Christmas Day 2005 as being Mr. Inside, while a social activist of great renown was shown as Mr. Outside." He was working against the system, from outside trying to make change, and I was sitting comfortably inside the system.

Actually, that couldn't be farther from the truth, because I work both outside and inside. And I would say to Professor Washington, while working outside, I've been active in my community, the East Garfield Park community, a blighted community, west of this location, in making things happen that are positive. For example, at our Dr. King Boys and Girls Club, we not only send kids to college on full scholarships, but we also train them how to behave once at college – that is, as problem-solvers. We pay for ACT and SAT testing at the King Boys and Girls Club, pull in kids from the local high schools and train them how to take the tests, and tell them how they should deport themselves once they get to college. And we keep up with them. We also give them mentors.

One girl was lucky enough to have a mentor who was the president of Diners Club, Brenda Gaines. This girl could call Brenda Gaines at any time and ask, Ms. Gaines, what should I do about this, or how do I approach this problem, etc.

We also deal with elementary school youngsters, because we're concerned about more than just recreation and filling spare time. That

---

[9] Dr. Christopher R. Reed is professor of history and formerly held the Seymour Logan Chair in North American History at Roosevelt University.

means I can tell Mr. Washington about having placed eight children in a private school up north where tuition runs $10,000 a year, with one about to graduate from the first class we placed. Now of course we have thousands of kids in Chicago – we have about 500,000 in the public school system – but I think every positive step forward is a major step forward. And when I talk like this, it makes me feel good even when I hear statistics that sort of dampen my spirits.

So I am Mr. Outside doing something, as well as being Mr. Inside doing historical studies. Also as Mr. Outside I would say I was the go-to guy for years when it came to confronting criminal elements in the neighborhood. With my large stature and fearful look (an exaggeration, to be sure), I was called on to confront gang-bangers, and I'm still here to talk about it, so I feel good about that. But that's just a preface. Now I'll talk about my role as Mr. Inside.

Introduction to Washington

I have been studying Booker T. Washington for about 40 years. I was introduced to Washington, being a northerner, through scholarship, because people didn't talk a lot about Booker T. Washington when I was coming along in the late 1940s and 1950s and 1960s. They talked about DuBois here and there, but not a lot about DuBois, either. This is when DuBois was about to die, in 1963, and Paul Robeson was fading, so there were new lights on the scene.

Learning about Booker T. Washington through August Meyers' classic study *Negro Thought in America, 1880-1915; Racial Ideologies in the Age of Booker T. Washington* (1963) in the 1960s introduced me to Washington and had me intrigued over what this man was all about. Within 10 years of Washington being discussed in *Negro Thought in America*, historian Louis Harlan wrote a multi-volume study on Washington using the Booker T. Washington papers at the Library of Congress that revealed even more about Booker T. Washington.

Research into Washington's role in African-American life, especially based on his manuscript files held at the Library of Congress, reveals that he indeed deserved to have an historical era named in his honor. For those that don't know, the period 1895-1915 is deemed the Era of Booker T. Washington. This is very appropriate for a very complex man with a strategic plan for national economic development. His was a strategic plan for African-Americans of all classes, so Washington contributed mightily to African-American liberation and still does so today.

Necessity for Economic Independence

Despite comments that there's nothing meaningful in history, or little that you can learn from history and apply, I would say that the direction that black Americans should take today towards advancement starts with an understanding of what Washington was all about. His personal experience – he lived through the Reconstruction of the South – provided him with an immediate realization that independence came through one's ability to take economic care of one's self and to do it with regularity.

What he saw during the Reconstruction period immediately following the Civil War was an inordinate amount of attention paid to politics and the personal advancement that it brought to individuals who held office. And that's something, unfortunately, that we see too much of today. So-and-so's got an office, so the problems of the race have been solved. Not so.

One of the things Washington knew, and others knew immediately after the Emancipation, was that the ownership of land should be of paramount importance, and that slaves had learned very well how important it was to till the soil and realize the dream of controlling the products of the soil. University of Maryland historian Ira Berlin's 1998 book *Many Thousands Gone: The First Two Centuries of Slavery in North America* outlines the slaves' economy, the control of the enslaved over as much of their food supply as they could muster during the oppressive days of slavery. This involved working one small plot of land while a slave, down in the quarter, sometimes sneaking away to do so, working one small plot of land and building a surplus which could be marketed in Mobile, New Orleans, Baltimore, Savannah, or Charleston. And the surplus, the money from the surplus, went into the pocket of the slave.

And what did the slave do with the surplus? Those who were quite frugal and quite sensible used it to purchase their freedom or the freedom of their loved ones. Some, of course, wasted their money.

According to Berlin, this caused masters to recognize that the best way to control slaves was to substitute for the slaves' economy a slaves' allowance. Under this arrangement, the slaves' allowance, the master supplied all that the slave needed. Sound familiar? This restricted the accumulation of capital and cut off an avenue to freedom and competition once Emancipation came.

Now, enough slaves had continued to involve themselves in the slaves' economy so that when Emancipation came the first thing these blacks did was try to build on what they had done during slavery, becoming business people and then entrepreneurs.

Washington and Higher Education

In the area of education, which Washington considered another economic asset, Washington promoted the primary importance of a particular type of training – vocational or industrial training – that he felt would lead an impoverished people out of economic dependency and into a place that competitively put them on a road to true equality. It was never a case of Washington condemning higher education; it was a matter of placing important things on a priority list for his times.

Let me share a little of Booker T. Washington from copies of his papers held at the Library of Congress. This is Washington in 1908 from a confidential note to a Mr. Whitefield McKinlay, who lived in Washington.

Mr. McKinlay:

Enclosed I send you a copy of a letter which I wish you would treat as confidential. I am sending it to you as a sample of what I am doing constantly to help young colored men through college. This of course is in the face of the charge that I try to hinder rather than help that kind of education. This young fellow [there was a recommendation included] is in the law school of Harvard University.

– Booker T. Washington

And, of course, we know that Washington's daughter, Portia, went to college in the North. Washington was not against higher education! But he understood that there was a need to set priorities. He had an awareness of national economic development. For a nation early in its period of independence, it is less efficient to build universities for the few young people that can benefit from university training; it is better to send them abroad. It's far cheaper to train 200 students abroad than to build a university for them. And it makes more sense to commit yourself to educating say, two to 20 million young people at home in grades one through eight, than to build a university that will be underpopulated.

That is the context in which Booker T. Washington's thinking should be understood. You have phases through which as a young society you should pass as you attempt to benefit your people. With education in Washington's time, it was a commitment to teaching skills that would get people jobs. Today, Booker T. Washington's plan would be likened to convincing Bill and Melinda Gates to invest in computer literacy – which they would do and are doing – over interpretive dance or skills in literary analysis so that we can increase the number of journalists in our community. Computer skills make more sense for the great mass of people, I think we'd all agree.

Practical Approach to Education

I have three sons who are all college-trained. The youngest was an honor student who studied international relations. When it came time to gain employment, he couldn't find anything in the Midwest – if you're in international relations, you have to go out East and get into a network that will allow you to enter the foreign service.

In his case, having followed the wrong path, he retooled himself and studied computers and ended up spending a lot of money as a certified Cisco engineer. I'm not saying he wasted four years in his studies, and I was quite proud of him, hearing him lecture to older people on foreign affairs, but I think there's something to a practical approach to education.

I'm planning to retire in 90 days, and when we went through over 100 applications to fill my slot, it was quite tragic to see how many people were going to be turned down, people who had doctorates, because there just aren't a lot of jobs in history. I guess I'll go on record saying I don't dissuade anybody from studying history, especially if they're from a wealthy family and don't have to worry about employment after they get their doctorate, but I do encourage them to think things out. There just aren't a lot of jobs, and there are a lot of cab drivers out there with this pedigree.

My other two sons, by the way, are in practical areas. The oldest son is in accounting, and the next oldest, a Marine Corps veteran, is in management, having studied public administration.

Washington began to think about the future of black America while the nation was in the industrial age and yet the South in which he lived was still in the pre-industrial age. Yes, there was some mining, there was some textile production over in North Carolina and other places, but basically the South was economically backward. So people down at Tuskegee were taught skills that were useful for the times. And we all know historically that the South didn't become mechanized until after World War I.

One of our leading historians, whom I admire greatly, criticized Washington for years because Washington didn't encourage students at Tuskegee to study engineering, as students up to the north were studying. Well, it made sense to study engineering if you could get into an engineering class, say at the University of Illinois or University of Michigan. The North was industrializing by the 1880s and 1890s, with monopoly capitalism emerging in the early twentieth century.

But the South was pre-industrial, so learning the skill of a blacksmith did make sense if you could shoe a horse and make a good living. And by the way, there were still blacksmiths in Chicago in 1900. The combustion engine did not take over in Chicago until World War I. You actually had blacks who were blacksmiths on State Street in the early 1900s.

Roads Toward Advancement

Bricklaying and brickmaking were important. Even domestic work was important and was taught down at Tuskegee. My mother was a domestic in the 1950s and rose to become vice president of a maid service about a mile north of this building, in one of the most exclusive areas of the city, the Gold Coast. The vice presidency that she held had her sending out maids by the late 1950s into these apartments where, as she would say, "the girls would hit the high spots." They weren't moving furniture, and they weren't doing back-breaking work; they were doing essential work providing essential services for professionals who didn't have time to dust, wash dishes, or make beds. This became a rather lucrative business. And by the way, the president running the business was an African-American woman with a college degree.

I'm going to read one other thing from a letter by Booker T. Washington, this one from 1909. You have to remember that Washington was condemned by members of the intellectual elite as being too limited to lead the race, too limited intellectually to develop a strategic plan that would help the masses out of the impoverishment in which they lived. And here is what Booker T. Washington wrote in 1909, with my own observations in brackets:

> Yes, go and visit the President. Go in a quiet way to President Taft and put before him your views regarding what he should do and what he should not do in reference to the colored people. [Now, this is not a timid man writing this! This is not passivity.] Of course, the committee of blacks that go to the President might begin by thanking him for what he has already said and done that is favorable. [That makes sense.] I have spoken to him plainly and frankly, giving him my views, but there is nothing like his being impressed from different angles and by different individuals. [Pretty shrewd.] This is the way white people make public sentiment. [Different angles, different individuals, different approaches, the person being bombarded gets the message.] This is the program we should pursue. We do a great deal of talking among ourselves, but little in the presence of the people whom we wish to influence.

That was Washington in 1909. Look at him carefully. I'm glad to see that he's being looked at anew today. There's a lot to learn from him, and I'm glad to see that he's part of your strategic plan for the twenty-first century. Thank you, Booker T. Washington.

Chapter 8

Washington the Visionary

Rev. William "Bill" Winston[10]

In my opinion, there has been a very subtle negative attachment to some of the contributions of Booker T. Washington, but I'd like people to think of him as a visionary. He was only the Moses that came before the Joshua. He was a person who had his part to play and to fulfill. He was not the answer for all time – he was an answer for his time. And he was a part of the continuum of history of the black race.

Washington played that part well. He came in at a time when the deep South was in abject poverty, and there was no hope for many people. When he gave his Atlanta speech, the first response was that the blacks saw a glimmer of hope, a belief that they could rise up from despair. His approach was captured in that famous line, "cast down your buckets where you are."

Well, in all of our lives there is genius. What he was trying to do was tap into the genius of the people of his time, to pull it out as a trade or a skill that they could use to prove themselves indispensable to society. And then they could raise themselves up and enable the next generation to take over from there.

I am a product of Booker T. Washington. The things that I have achieved in my life, in every place that I have gone, have been at the top of the rung. Top gun, top salesman, so forth and so on. I learned that from his legacy. I studied him like I would study anyone that I'm interested in. We have in Chicago one of the top ministries in the country – he put that kind of excellence in me.

Unfortunately, there has been a conspiracy to destroy the historical legacy of the black race and specifically of Booker T. Washington. For example, the Black Wall Street of the early twentieth century in Tulsa, Oklahoma had more black millionaires than had ever been together in the United States, but looking at the site today, you can't even tell it's ever been

---

[10] Rev. William "Bill" S. Winston is founder and pastor of Living Word Christian Center, a 15,000-member church located in Forest Park, Illinois.

there. How about the Tuskegee Airmen? Consider Tuskegee Army Air Field in Alabama: It has been plowed under. They didn't even leave the remnants for a museum. There has been a conspiracy to conceal this great man's legacy.

Economic Leadership

Now, DuBois had his approach to black advancement, but so did Booker T. Washington. And I think people fail to understand they appealed to different segments of the black community. I think a person can have friends who are both Republicans and Democrats, and it won't hurt them at all. So, as we look at this, I'm not just following behind the masses. What I'm doing is picking out a part for myself and saying, this is what fits me best, and I take that and put it in my life and make it work.

I think sometimes we need to change our paradigm of how we see people. Washington went inside of a person and pulled out what he or she was capable of achieving, changing that person from the inside out. In our ministry here in Chicago, what I'm trying to do is to change a person on the inside, through my teachings, and then that person will go back and change their community. I think that's what Booker T. Washington was saying: Send me your people, send me your tired, send me your hopeless, send me all the poor, and what I'm going to do is to put skills and ambition in them, so that when I send them out, they're going to change the communities they go to. That is what he had, and it is his legacy.

That brings us to the economic side of Washington's philosophy. You can march, sit at forbidden lunch counters, and so forth, and sure enough you'll get some push-back. But when you hit that economic demon, that's when people who have never opposed you before will lift their hand against you. Once you start accomplishing things and making a way for a group of people who have not had a part of this economic life and power, all of a sudden you get a lot of push-back, and it's very, very subtle.

When we were trying to purchase the shopping mall that we have now – it's a 33-acre shopping mall – the majority of people on the village board that were controlling everything didn't want us to have it. One of the biggest reasons they didn't want us to have it was because they felt that black people coming in there really couldn't help that community much at all.

Now, I understand that racism is going to be here when I'm gone, so that doesn't bother me. But to make a concerted effort and go downtown to change the zoning laws so that I can't buy a mall – there's a reason for that. I talked to the majority of big banks in Chicago and they refused to give us a loan to purchase the property. They said, "We're not in the church business." And I said, "This ain't a church, man. I'm talking about business. We're putting businesses in here; this is a business. I have a business background, and I have people on the board who are business people, lawyers and so forth." But they never would loan us the money.

So I went to a black bank. That black bank didn't have the money themselves, so they participated the loan out and got other black banks to participate. People will stand in line to loan us money now.

Something happens when economics come in. I'm not against the political approach, but I don't want to sit at the lunch counter – I want to own it. Ownership is what Booker T. Washington started talking about, and that is when he began to be demonized. Then everybody began to talk about him. That undercurrent is something we still have to fight today.

Booker T. Washington has fruit, and the Bible says you will know them by their fruit. You can go to Tuskegee right now, and it's still one of the finest universities in any country. Booker T. Washington has affected a whole lot of people's lives, and he has created leadership.

PART 3

ENTREPRENEURSHIP AND ECONOMIC DEVELOPMENT

Chapter 9

Adjustment to Society

John Sibley Butler[11]

I am going to focus on black entrepreneurship and economic development in Booker T. Washington's life and works.

I have chosen to look at Booker T. Washington in a way that is both academic and practical. Academically we can talk about two ways ethnic groups adjust to American society: through entrepreneurship and the education of children, and through working in factories.

Booker T. Washington's legacy has allowed the development within black America of a group that is very similar to other groups in American history who in response to discrimination, turned to entrepreneurship and self-help. Examples include Eastern European Jews, the Ibo in Africa, and Japanese and Cubans who moved to America.

Washington developed a group of black Americans who (a) have been educated for three, four, five, six generations; (b) have never known poverty; (c) have never lived in the ghettos of a city; and (d) have taken their way of life throughout America. In the academic setting, we call these "middlemen groups."

---

[11] Dr. John Sibley Butler holds the Gale Chair in Entrepreneurship and Small Business in the Graduate School of Business at the University of Texas at Austin.

Two Traditions of Black America

By the time I came of age as a high school senior in 1965 (my counselor went to Tuskegee), black Americans had already developed a strong tradition of education, and Charles Johnson's great book on the Negro college graduate had been published in 1947. These black Americans were already in their third generation of college matriculation. But how was it done? It was done through the application of business enterprises.

The data show that these successful blacks – we can call them the children of Booker T. Washington – more resemble the Jewish group in America, not the Irish group. They more resemble the Mormons in America, not the Italian group. They more resemble the Ibo in Africa, and not other groups. Those groups that were denied opportunity in America but who turned to entrepreneurship and created business enterprises, have always educated their children.

When we line up the data today and look at where the most educated people are, they're in the group that concentrates on entrepreneurship and self-help. Their parents, grandparents, and great-grandparents were self-employed and created a value structure that lasted throughout the generations.

If your great-great-grandparents worked in factories and you became a union person, then the idea was to work a great union job and to send your kids to a great union job. If your parents started a small shop, the probability of going to college was great.

The entrepreneurial tradition starts in Philadelphia and the early northern cities of the free blacks who predated Booker T. Washington. In Philadelphia and New York City, blacks had already organized business enterprises as free blacks during and even before the Civil War. We know there was legislative hostility.

One of the first entrepreneur pamphlets was developed in 1883. It was written by Dr. Henry Minton (1831-1895), who was the primary founder of the Boulé (the first African-American fraternity in the United States) and helped create a business district in Philadelphia before the Civil War. He and his associates concentrated on what Booker T. Washington would call, "what you can count and what you can do."

When I want to see the children of Booker T. Washington now, I turn to the Africans and Asians in my class who are likely to become entrepreneurs. Most of these groups, by the way, have never associated politics with doing well. The whole idea was to take it to the market, especially for Eastern European Jews and the Mormons in America.

So if you ask where is wealth in America, it's among certain parts of the population, not the entire white population. And as the children of Booker T. Washington come to America – whether it's the most recent Chinese or other groups – then what you learn is that wealth, of course, is related to entrepreneurship.

Interest in Wealth Creation

I have a friend who just finished a big study on Silicon Valley. Forty percent of all the entrepreneurs and wealth creators in Silicon Valley were Chinese and Indians. Americans have produced relatively few such companies themselves – it is the immigrants who are creating jobs and creating wealth. I know nobody who came to America to vote. Everybody who came to America was concerned with wealth creation.

Within America, we have black Americans in the tradition of Booker T. Washington who are much more similar to the entrepreneurial immigrant groups. I'm a fourth generation college graduate, from Louisiana, and in my church, since 1901, 99.4 percent of all the kids have gone to college.

So what does that mean? It means the values that Booker T. Washington generated have been maintained by a segment of the black population, and as they have moved across the country they have carried that value structure with them. And what are those values that Booker T. Washington left us? They are very similar to those held by other self-help groups. If you really want to see the children of Booker T. Washington, you should look at the Nigerians, you should look at the African students, where the entire emphasis is on doing well, and it comes from their parents.

Declining Values

Entrepreneurial African-Americans are more likely to be Southern in origin, because of the institution-building that took place there. In addition, they have a strong tradition of family college matriculation, not just one person. And finally, they have a strong history of economic stability. Now, it's hard to talk about wealthy blacks in America, because people will say, "Well, you just wait; things are going to get bad."

But why should that happen? The real problem is that the world of black America is upside down. All of the elements that are doing well in America have always done so by taking their problems to the market, but that attitude tends to be lost over time. America is a country where the first generation does well, in terms of entrepreneurship; the second generation struggles to go to college; the third generation has all kinds of issues; and the fourth generation is just not worth a damn.

So you have to struggle against that. At this point I'm director of the IC2 Institute at the University of Texas. We have an incubator, and we have created wealth. Michael Dell came through the institute. We have created more than 62 companies. Six have gone public, and 37 have been acquired. The most valuable of these was MetroWorks, which was acquired for $71 million, and the lowest was worth about $5 million. That's just what Booker T. Washington did at Tuskegee – that is, figuring out how you find wealth in a peanut and commercialize it.

So what we've done at Texas is take the Tuskegee model and create something in Austin, Texas that's very different from anything else. The

Silicon Valley model is also a contribution of Booker T. Washington and George Washington Carver. So the children of Booker T. Washington continue to step forward and turn the world right-side up.

Striving for Excellence

I see the contribution of Booker T. Washington throughout the nation. Wherever I go, I see people who understand the importance of entrepreneurship, the importance of markets, the importance of family, and the importance of creating things. But in the upside-down world of black America, all of the images are about the ghettoization of communities, about what people cannot do, about where people are.

The New York Times called me and said, let's talk about black men. And I said, let's talk about Morehouse. I'm on the research board at Morehouse. I want you to go down there and see what they're doing. Or let's talk about the Piney Woods. What you have to do is make heroes out of the individuals who know how to fly airplanes. If I'm interested in doing well, I should ask people, what have you done? If I'm interested in flying a helicopter, I should ask people how they fly it.

What we've got to do is capture and teach the best practices of people, in the Booker T. Washington tradition, who know how to do things. We must remember that less than a third of black America is in poverty, and less than a third of black America is not doing well. And we must also remember that the best school in Alabama, by any measure, is Tuskegee. It isn't the University of Alabama – Alabama is trying to do what Tuskegee did years ago in terms of technology transfer and wealth creation.

I think that the contribution of Booker T. Washington is still here.

Chapter 10

Moses in the Wilderness

Hycel Taylor, Ph.D.[12]

For the past four or five years, I've been traveling back and forth to Israel. Israel, as you well know, is a part of Africa. In fact, before the Suez Canal, it was an extension of Africa. I went there to try to get some vision of what this theme might mean in terms of creativity. I went to Mount Nebo, because I wanted to stand where Moses stood on that mountain. And Moses was there, as you well know, dealing with a people who had been in slavery for 400 years and then had to get them across that Red Sea and into that wilderness experience.

It was in that wilderness that creativity had to occur, where something different had to be done. How do you take a people out of 400 years of slavery, who had been conditioned, indoctrinated into all the negative things that life can offer, and bring them into what he called the Promised Land? Moses had to do something extraordinary. He didn't just bring them directly out of the Red Sea to the Promised Land. He stopped along the way ... to do some things that I think Booker T. Washington also did.

First of all, he brought them to Mt. Sinai. And when you read the Bible about Mt. Sinai, you are not merely reading about some laws that came down from the heavens conjured by Cecil B. DeMille. You are talking about a man who looked at his people and said, "I've got to do something that will transform them, that will make them a different kind of people on their way to the Promised Land."

And I think the most creative aspect of Booker T. Washington is that he himself is the paradigm we have to look at. He was a model of creativity. His life was a life that transformed itself into something that was extraordinary. He knew how to pat the lion, and to tell that lion "be cool"

---

[12] Rev. Dr. Hycel Taylor is founder and Senior Pastor of The Christian Life Fellowship, a holistic and interdenominational ministry in Skokie, Illinois.

until I get into a position where I can make a difference in the world. This is what made him creative.

Need for Change

And I think now as never before we need to look at his life not so much in terms of debates over whether he was conservative or liberal, or whether he had a debate with DuBois over the talented tenth – it's got nothing to do with that! He was not a conservative, and he was not a liberal. He was a black man trying to do something and to make a difference in the world out here.

This is his message: If you decide that you want to change the world, change yourself! Don't look at the world out there. What he taught us is that you've got to change yourself. Gandhi said, if you want to change the world, you change, and then let the world adjust to you.

Booker T. Washington was a man who teaches us all to be a man or a woman. He was a creative genius. He was able to take nothing and make something out of it. He was able to take a life and to build upon that life. And then the world had to adjust to him.

Chapter 11

The Value of Entrepreneurship

Gary MacDougal[13]

I'm a fan of Booker T. Washington because he believed in self-reliance, not government programs.

All my life, I've been an entrepreneur. I started an effort to build a company that ended up in the Fortune 1000, after coming out of school in debt, so I understand the entrepreneurial path, although I did not have the barriers to that path that many African-Americans have. I value entrepreneurship and I see it as a core value of our country, a great land of opportunity.

What do the following four companies have in common: American Express, one of the largest financial institutions in the world; TimeWarner, one of the top media companies in the world; Merrill Lynch, one of the top financial companies in the world; and Symantec, one of the two biggest software companies in the world? You know what they all have in common? They all have black CEOs. I have met them all. None of them is in their job because of affirmative action. All of them are in their jobs because they are the most qualified people the boards of directors of those companies could find to run those companies. And all of them are doing outstanding jobs.

Things are changing in this country. I would assert that there is no more ceiling of the type we used to talk about for blacks, or for women either. However, we've got a long way to go, because you need fertile ground in order to grow entrepreneurs. And that means people starting out and learning what I call the "soft skills" in life.

I pumped gas and cleaned restrooms as my entry-level job. It taught me to show up on time, take direction, and how to work. I worked in the cash economy, mowing lawns and babysitting. Did you know that 15 percent of the economy is a cash economy? And I think this is just fine, even though

---

[13] Gary MacDougal, is the author of *Make a Difference – A Spectacular Breakthrough in the Fight Against Poverty* (St. Martin's Press, 2000).

we talk about it in disparaging terms as "unreported income" and so forth. There is no tax up to $25,000 a year in income, so why should you fill out paperwork when you're doing small jobs? The cash economy is a big, big thing in the black community.

Building Economic Foundations

The statistics on black unemployment, blacks living in poverty, the number of young black men in jail and coming out of jail every day, are shocking indications that, for whatever reasons, the black community has yet to create a sound economic foundation, a base from which entrepreneurs can grow. I've been helping to reform welfare by guiding former welfare recipients into employment, and working to help guide ex-offenders, having paid their dues, back into a productive part of the economy.

Let me first say just a few things about welfare. Victor Hugo said there's nothing more powerful in the world than an idea whose time has come. And my idea is that there is no necessary reason why anyone in the United States of America should be on welfare. We have a great economy, we have plenty of money in the system to help disadvantaged people, and most people want to work.

My book, *Make a Difference*, describes my experience in chairing the governor's task force for human services reform in Illinois, where we reduced welfare rolls from 650,000 recipients to 85,000 recipients. That's an 86 percent reduction, 85 percent in Cook County, which William Julius Wilson regarded as "ground zero" for this challenge. Most of those who left welfare are working, and most are working above the minimum wage. My book describes that process, how that happened.

My view is that this should happen in each and every state, and I have been devoting my time to going around the country talking to governors, talking to anybody who'll listen, about why we now know what it takes to move people from welfare to work, and that therefore there's no excuse for having people left on welfare rolls.

Success of Welfare Reform

Those who say welfare reform was not a success nationally don't really understand or are in denial. Nationally, the rolls went from 12.5 million down to 4.5 million. If that's not a good measure of success, I don't know what is. There are those who say it's because we've had a great economy, but the welfare rolls have not gone down in previous good economies. They have gone down since 1996, when Congress passed welfare reform.

Work is the centerpiece of a happy life. At UPS, where I'm a director, we've hired 60,000 people off of the welfare rolls, and guess what we've found: They have lower turnover than anybody else. That is enlightened self-interest; it's a good business risk.

I was at a meeting where a woman who had been on welfare for 15 years spoke. She had gotten off welfare. She worked for UPS for three years and became a manager, and she is now a stockholder. This is what it's all about.

Illinois is leading the way, and other efforts are going on. We've persuaded Gov. Bob Riley in Alabama to set up a task force. The principles of reforming welfare systems are integrating the services – you can't have a system so complex that people need a Ph.D. in order to figure out how to get help. You can't do it without connecting the private sector. You can't do it without connecting schools, local governments, United Ways, and the Chambers of Commerce. And you have to measure outcomes. Unlike most government programs, where outputs are not measured, moving people from welfare to work in Illinois and in other states is starting to get measured.

Poverty Programs Well-Financed

It's not about money. Anybody who tells you we need more money for poor people doesn't understand the situation. We are now spending, as a nation, at the federal and state level, $400 billion a year to help people below the poverty line. That is about $10,000 per person in poverty, $40,000 for a family of four; the poverty line is $18,000. So we could just convert it all to cash and everybody would be out of poverty. So anybody who tells you we need more money for programs for poverty, you can tell them they're wrong.

And it's not about available jobs. There are 11 million illegal immigrants in this country, and most of them are working. Where do you think those jobs come from? They come from desperate employers who very much need somebody to make those beds and to work in those kitchens and on those construction sites. And they don't want to hire illegal immigrants, but they need to get that work done. If they hire illegals, they could get in trouble themselves. They would much rather hire someone else. So anybody who tells you the big problem is no jobs, you can tell them that's nonsense.

There is plenty of money and plenty of jobs, but we still have 4.5 million people on welfare. There's something wrong with that picture – and we can fix it. My goal is to have fewer than a million people on welfare in the next few years, and I'm working with a lot of key people to try to make that happen.

Jobs for Ex-Offenders

Let me turn to another subject that's tied in with this. Did you know that more than 600,000 people are coming out of the nation's prisons this year? These are people who have paid their dues. Most of these people have kids on welfare. If you talk to people on welfare or in bad neighborhoods, most of them know somebody who is connected with the prison system – either in prison, on parole, or involved in the justice system in some way. This is a tragedy, and this shouldn't be.

When offenders come out of prison, they shouldn't be sentenced to a street corner for the rest of their lives because of insurmountable barriers to jobs. What you owe them – once they've paid their dues and only when they've paid their dues – is a chance to reconnect with the world, to have a job, and to go on and live a life. And that is not happening in this country, because like so many other things the government is making the problem worse.

Jeb Bush, who is one of the smartest, most capable governors in this country, who cares deeply about people, engaged us to set up in Florida the first statewide task force on ex-offenders. Twenty-six thousand ex-offenders are coming out of prison in Florida this year, most into about eight communities.

The state of Florida creates barriers to about a third of the jobs in the state, through licensing, regulations, and restrictions on what ex-offenders can and can't do. Gov. Bush came out with the first executive order to direct all state agencies to "clean house" on this and remove unnecessary barriers. This idea has been picked up by California, New York, and Minnesota. We're going state by state by state.

In addition to such an executive order, each ex-offender needs to connect with some competent, successful adult. Going right back into his old circle of friends is not going to do it. Where do the mentors come from? If you ask people in Florida who is going to take the job of being a sounding board, being a mentor for an ex-offender, they'll tell you it's the churches. Gov. Bush is very supportive of faith-based solutions, and our program will probably be getting 95 percent of our mentors out of the churches in Florida.

Enlightened Self-Interest

So there are answers to these problems. I think that before we're going to get marriage in the black community at a higher rate, we're going to have to have successful men. These women are too smart to marry men who are hanging out on the street corner. They want to marry men who are going to contribute to the family, are going to have jobs.

So we'll be meeting with employers and talking to them about the enlightened self-interest of hiring ex-offenders. We have a meeting on the south side of Chicago coming up with the top executives of UPS and the Community Federation of Grand Boulevard about hiring ex-offenders.

The interesting thing about this ex-offender work is that once the ex-offender has the job, you don't want to know who he or she is. You don't want them labeled. I know that one of the ex-offenders for whom we've obtained employment at UPS in metro Chicago is a manager, but they won't tell me who it is. And that's the way it should work.

Daniel Burnham said, "Make no small plans." So I have a goal: that there will be fewer than a million people on the welfare rolls nationwide before I check out. And my other goal is to have a program in each state so that ex-offenders can connect with a competent, caring adult and a job.

Chapter 12

Generational Crossroads

Charles Horne, Ph.D.[14]

I grew up with many role models. Booker T., George Washington Carver, Frederick Douglass, Marcus Garvey – many of those folks were my role models. When I grew up, we talked about them in school, on the streets, and in the barbershops. We had people we could try to emulate to get to the next position in life.

Black Americans today have many different attitudes. We have traditionalists, conservatives, liberals, pre-moderns, postmoderns, and people with no intellectual attitudes at all. We all seem to be marching to our own individual drumbeat. I conclude that we need greater unity of principle and purpose, which would lead to economic self-sufficiency and self-determination.

Black Human Capital

In Chicago, in the South Shore neighborhood, gentrification is taking place like you've never seen before. South Shore is a jewel for the black community in Illinois, and yet many of the pilgrims who created it are allowing it to disappear. I'm not blaming anybody, and I'm not chastising anybody. But if you lose that jewel through gentrification and revitalization and you don't own it, then something is wrong with that picture. It's a sad state.

Pittsburgh used to have a population of 750,000 people. Now it's 300,000 or less. Half of the property is up for sale at 30 cents on the dollar. If we were smart, and not so intellectual, we'd be buying Pittsburgh.

In a harbor in Maryland, there used to be urban blight. Now it's worth a gazillion dollars. But we didn't have the wherewithal to take advantage of that. Seattle, Philadelphia, Houston ... I could go on and on and on.

---

[14] Dr. Charles Horne is president of the Pacific Northwest Chapter of the National Black Chamber of Commerce.

But we have an opportunity today. There must be a universal connecting of the dots, by all of us. You need to know what's going on in Seattle, you need to know what's going on in Dallas, Atlanta, Chicago, Detroit, and so on.

Al Sharpton, Michael Dyson, Tavis Smiley, Lee Walker, all of us need to be connected one to another. As a people, we must operationalize black human capital. We're all valuable. We're very valuable, one to another. We must operationalize black human capital – intellectual capital, financial capital – and commit ourselves to improved levels of financial literacy.

I know a lot of times when I'm giving speeches people say, "What do you mean by financial literacy?" People don't know anything about the financial infrastructure. We don't know what the fed rate is, what our credit scores are, the difference between capital formation and a capital platform, anything about investment strategies, or even anything about trading. Money is a commodity. You buy it, and you sell it. That's what it is. And many of us are not aware of what that means.

Money may not be everything, but it's way out in front of whatever's running second. We need to keep that in mind. We must remember the Golden Rule: He who has the gold, makes the rules. We need to keep these little clichés in mind when we discuss these issues.

Laws of Necessity

We need to understand the laws of necessity. We are driven by two factors, whether we like it or not. Number one is need, and the other one is greed. You are driven by need or greed. Bill Gates is a product of the Pacific Northwest. He started with $600. That's the story they tell. But his dad had a gazillion dollars. So, Bill Gates went into his garage and he created all of these technological advances, but he also created an institution – a stock company. And he and Paul Allen held all the stock. So when the product became valuable, his stock was valuable. How much stock do we have in our businesses?

We must embrace an attitude of mental wealth, to focus collectively on the commercialization of our black communities and create an atmosphere of self-sufficiency, whereby dollars are circulated through our communities more than one time. The primary market, the secondary market, and the tertiary market – the wealth must generate and go through our community at least three times.

There is little doubt that we as a people suffer from many and varied social inequities. But this cliché should never deter us from our quest for economic justice. In light of our earning and consumption strength – some $800 billion – we can no longer make excuses for the economic plight of our people.

We must recognize that we consume 95 percent of what we make. And we must bury the other 5 percent, because it's not in the investment community. Somebody said we invest less than 1.2 percent. That's egregious.

Transition to Wealth

But we can transition our people and our income and our wealth. Just because you have a political persuasion different from mine does not mean we cannot come together for the common good of our people.

There are 26 pretty reputable black banks across the country. And in some quarters we are excited about the 26 banks, but that's nothing to be proud of. With the population we have in this country, we have only 26 banks – and many of them are not corresponding banks, they're simply pass-through banks for other corresponding institutions. You have four in Washington, DC, three in Los Angeles, two in Atlanta. This is not something we should shout about.

At the end of the day, there has to be a wake-up call to all black Americans. I leave you with these five observations:

(1) As a people we need to establish unified and collective procurement and purchasing processes and activities. We need to own our own supply companies.

(2) We need to create and implement community development financial institutions and commercial banks. How can you follow the money if you don't know where it is? We need to have our own system of financing our businesses. We need to investigate banking policies and procedures relative to redlining and greenlining. Before gentrification takes place, many of our communities are redlined: They will not loan money, and they will not place a bank in that community.

(3) We need to support black businesses and entrepreneurship.

(4) We need to invest in media TV and radio. Al Sharpton is syndicated now. But we need to do a lot more of that.

(5) And in closing, I'll read just one paragraph. This comes from the Declaration of Economic Independence of African-Americans of the United States:

> We the people of African descent, who now reside and have petitioned to reside within the boundaries of these United States and its territories, and in order to participate in a more perfect Union, obtain economic justice, secure financial independence, ensure domestic tranquility, and provide for the common enhancement of all African-Americans and promote the general welfare of the African-American nation, we do ordain and establish that we will continue to pursue life, liberty, and the pursuit of property.

PART 4

TOWARD A MORE ACCURATE HISTORY

Chapter 13

Overstated Conflict

William B. Allen, Ph.D.[15]

The question of the hour is the question of education, and in particular the achievement gap. To talk about that, though, it is necessary to put it in context, even in some degree of relationship to Booker T. Washington.

I make it a habit, when I'm talking about W.E.B. DuBois, to quote Booker T. Washington always, and I make it a habit, typically, when I'm talking about Booker T. Washington, to quote W.E.B. DuBois.

I do this because I'm of the opinion that the division between them is exaggerated. This is not to say they weren't of different opinions in some important respects. After all, Booker T. Washington contributed enduring institutions and ideas that have a life, that seem to have an assured existence even well beyond our own time. He never fell into the vulnerabilities that came ultimately to characterize DuBois. But with regard to the fundamental question, the question of education, I believe the division is overstated.

DuBois cites Booker T. Washington quite approvingly when describing the capacities of the freed slaves, the remarkable activities that transpired in the aftermath of slavery, and the establishment of schools throughout the South. Individual citizens, young and old, took themselves into schoolrooms or schoolhouses or makeshift school sites, acquiring the rudiments of learning and reading – immediately, of course, in order to gain access to their Bibles; at length, in order to perfect those instrumentalities

---

[15] Dr. William B. Allen is professor of political science at Michigan State University.

that had been unnaturally and prematurely foreshortened during the experience of slavery.

It was also the case that Booker T. Washington typically cited W.E.B. DuBois. In *The Future of the American Negro*, he is particularly at pains to cite DuBois to show how little the two of them disagree:

> The Negro should be taught that material development is not an end, but simply a means to an end. As Professor W.E.B. DuBois puts it, "the idea should not simply be to make men carpenters, but to make carpenters men." The Negro has a highly religious temperament, but what he needs more and more is to be convinced of the importance of weaving his religion and morality into the practical affairs of daily life.

Respect for Intellectual Achievements

Those who think Booker T. Washington is merely the forerunner of vocational education as it was widely practiced through public institutions in the United States are wrong. While some of the architects of vocational education may have cited Washington, they have misapplied his thinking. They may have cited statements he made about the inappropriateness of devoting study to Latin and Greek when other necessities remained to be completed, but they are mistaken if in doing so they suggest Washington meant to denigrate the importance of intellectual accomplishment. Booker T. Washington was no less an intellectual than was W.E.B. DuBois.

Indeed, it is fair to say that what is particularly important about Washington in terms of the discussion with DuBois is to observe that his ultimate aim, even as expressed in the quotation I just read, is no less intellectually ambitious than was the aim of W.E.B. DuBois. Washington sought to inspire the sense of accomplishment that could fuel the ambition of the most talented souls no matter what their numbers might be. And he did so in a way that was best calculated to achieve the end – not through exhortation, but through raising the standard of emulation, using accomplishment from the least level and the most immediately practical all the way up to the most theoretical.

Do not fail to understand that the accomplishments of George Washington Carver were theoretical. Sure, we use the products of the peanut, but his true accomplishment was an intellectual accomplishment, a theoretical accomplishment. And this is what Booker T. Washington sought to foster as he left Hampton – as a very young man, remember – in order to found an institution of higher learning. He did this in a community in which the bridge between lower learning and higher learning had not yet been established, and therefore had to do so by creating the lower and the higher in the same motion, and having to draw out all the primary and intermediate steps before ascending to the peak, to the mountaintop. But it was the mountaintop that Booker T. Washington envisioned.

Intellectual exceptionality was no less the goal for Washington than it was for DuBois. The other conversations, the political conversations – those are secondary. The real question Washington poses for us is this: What do you have in you? Call it a question of character if you want, but it's also a question of ability.

Achievement Gap

Now with respect to the achievement gap, how do we apply this? Let us just remember that we call it an achievement gap. This is a recent accomplishment. Until a few years ago, we called it the racial gap.

I brought the people from the ACT college testing service into my office in Virginia when they had produced their report in 1998 and described the racial gap that once again had appeared in their findings after students had taken the test. I belabored them over the terminology, persuaded as I was that what we decide to call a thing determines how we think about it.

I asked, "Is it a racial gap when you find Americans typically perform less well than Asian students?" They never called that a racial gap. They didn't acknowledge it as a racial gap. They agreed with me that it was just an achievement gap. I said, therefore, then is it not equally true that when American black youngsters perform less well than any other youngsters, that too is equally an achievement gap?

The reason to be concerned about this is not to score points in the struggle over racial identity or the battle over recognition or the assertion of self-importance. The reason to pay attention to this is because you can't solve the problem if you don't know what it is. Once we realize we're talking about an achievement gap, then we can speak meaningfully about the educational procedures required to be followed in order to alleviate it. We can then respond to Clifford Adelman, who demonstrates that the course-taking pattern has more to do with performance on standardized tests than any other single factor. Students in poor schools who do not get college preparatory curricula do not fare well. Duh! Who's surprised? It's not a racial gap; it's an achievement gap.

But that same gap stares us in the face, forcing us to ask why we sustain it, why we maintain it, what about our society makes it possible, and why we have not so organized our resources in order to solve that problem. Glenn Loury posed that question in his own manner last evening. He asked, "Can't you teach your children?" And that is the proper question.

The achievement gap, then, ultimately is a question of the failure to teach, not a question of the children's failure to learn. And as we drive that point into our consciousness, and we take deeper responsibility for it, we will be less patient with all those who merely pretend to teach. We will not stand on the sidelines leaving them free to pretend, when we know they accomplish nothing. And therefore we will agree, as Washington has given us the model, that we care a lot more about testing people to identify failure than we do about reconfirming a sense of self-importance.

Need for High Expectations

I've always observed that we are utterly uncompromising when it comes to athletics. We know the pathway to success – that is, to push the athlete to the point of failure. That's how you produce the best athlete. Academics is no different. To get the best academics, the best intellects, they must be pushed to the point of failure. This is not a thing to be dreaded; it is a thing to be pined for. If we accept anything less than that, we've failed them.

Thus, the achievement gap, as a broad social issue, a broad social question, is precisely the question Washington was addressing, but look at the difference in context. Washington addressed it as someone who had just escaped slavery, speaking to people who had just left slavery. He was affirming their capacities while acknowledging the measure of the task that lay before them.

Today we do not have that excuse. It has been a long, long time. To a student not very long ago who was waxing on too long about the legacy of slavery and how it holds him back, as he sat in the classroom in front of me, I said, "Take off your coat." So he took off his coat. Then I said, "Take off your shirt." He looked at me, but he took off his shirt. He went on, constantly complaining and protesting. And I said, "Take off your t-shirt." He was going to stop there, because he didn't know what I was up to. He protested. I said, "Take it off!" And he said, "Why, professor?" I said, "I want to see the stripes on your back. If you don't have them, don't claim them."

The achievement gap is a product of allowing people to claim what they have no title to. It is reinforced by the affirmative action, welfare mentality, when we should demand that people push to the point of failure.

Chapter 14

The Washington-DuBois Tension

Mark Bauerlein, Ph.D.[16]

I shall get to the achievement gap in a moment, but I want to follow up on some of Professor Allen's comments about the DuBois-Washington tension – to the historical record on that relationship.

In 1895, DuBois had left school. He had gone through Fisk, Harvard, and Germany, and he was setting out on a career as an academic, researcher, and teacher. He applied to a few schools asking for jobs, including Washington's.

DuBois wrote to Washington saying, I would like to come to Tuskegee and begin my employment there. I'm a Fisk graduate, and these are my qualifications.

DuBois was, obviously, one of the most trained young students in the country at this time. But he was an unknown, writing to Washington, the most famous educator, African-American or white, in the country. A month went by, and Washington was very busy, but when he did get back to DuBois a month later he accepted him for a post at Tuskegee and wrote offering terms.

DuBois in the meantime had received an offer from Wilberforce University, and he took it quickly. He was desperate to find employment. And so he honorably wrote back to Washington about the position, saying, I've already accepted a post at Wilberforce, and that was that.

Washington's Respect for DuBois

A couple of years later, DuBois is at Wilberforce, and he's unhappy. He dislikes what he considers the religiosity of the school, and he's also engaged to a student at Wilberforce. And so he thinks, I want to make a change. He writes to Washington again asking him for an opening at Tuskegee.

---

[16] Dr. Mark Bauerlein is professor of English at Emory University.

Washington writes to him more quickly this time and agrees. He says, let's talk, let's come to terms; we'd like to have you here. DuBois writes back and says, something has come up. I've been offered a one-year fellowship at the University of Pennsylvania to do research; can we delay this for a year?

DuBois goes up to Penn and is very unhappy there. He recalls later that he never really got integrated into the life of the college. He does some important research in Philadelphia, but during that year he gets another offer, from Atlanta University. He decides to take it, preferring Atlanta to Tuskegee at the time.

A few more years pass, DuBois feels restless again, and he writes to Washington once more, asking him about an opening at Tuskegee. Washington again agrees. But then another thing comes up; there is an opening for the D.C. school superintendent position. DuBois thinks maybe this would actually be a better fit for him than Tuskegee, and he makes still another request, asking Washington to write a letter of recommendation for the job. Washington actually does write a letter, not a strong letter, but any letter from Booker T. Washington carries more weight than just about anything in the United States at this time for a post open to African-Americans.

Some of Washington's lieutenants in Washington, D.C. write him and say, don't support DuBois for this; there are other, better people, more devoted to him, for the job. Washington holds off but doesn't cancel his support. Nevertheless, someone totally unrelated to the jockeying was hired for the position.

DuBois had made three requests of Washington, and three times Washington complied. He clearly respected DuBois's intellectual abilities and was willing to back him.

Intervening for DuBois

A few other things are worth noting here. When DuBois was pulled out of a sleeping car on the Southern Railway at the turn of the century, he filed a lawsuit against the railway for this discrimination in interstate movement, and he asked Washington for help. Washington responded, I will support you, I will give you the financial support for this so long as there is nothing in writing and I can hand the cash to you directly, hand to hand. And he did. He actually asked some of the leaders of the Southern Railway about their policy, to see if he could intervene. One of them was a descendant of Abraham Lincoln, but they fended him off.

Another fact to remember: DuBois published *The Souls of Black Folk*, with that notorious chapter on Washington, in 1903 – if you read the textbooks, this is considered the decisive break with Washington, and from then on there was a sharp division. The book came out in spring of that year.

A few months later, though, DuBois was in the Washington home in Tuskegee having dinner. This was because he was teaching summer school at Tuskegee at that time. Washington was quite forbearing about the intellectual differences with DuBois, and at this point the cooperative relationship was still in place.

Washington did believe in DuBois's intellectual strengths, and he did know there were differences between them, but so long as DuBois did not side with Washington's enemies, such as Monroe Trotter, if he didn't align himself, if he retained some independence, Washington could live with that and could work in cooperation with DuBois.

DuBois felt the same way. When DuBois did a conference, as he did annually in Atlanta on Negro crime in Georgia, Washington came. DuBois gave an introductory speech honoring Washington's work.

So while there were guarded feelings in terms of intellectual differences, the institutional connections were quite strong. And I think in terms of those earlier 10 years, in which Washington showed himself quite open to intellectual dissent – not institutional dissent, but intellectual dissent – he is to be credited for that.

Persistent Achievement Gap

Now, regarding the achievement gap between the races, let me give you some numbers on one area of it.

In terms of reading scores over the years, since the early 1970s there has been a significant closure of the gap, but the numbers haven't been so strong in the past few years. There were great gains among African-American students during the 1980s, and that's a reflection of more students having access to better schools, and more students going to college.

Among nine-year-olds, fourth graders, we have seen improvement. In 1999 on the NAEP exam – the nation's report card – in reading there was a 35-point gap between white and black students. That narrowed to 26 points in 2004. That's good news.

If we move up to eighth grade, we also see some significant improvement from 1999 to 2004. The score gap decreased from 29 points to 22 points. If you look at a longer range of years, however, it's not that great, because in 1990 it was 21 points. It widened in the 1990s and has gotten a little closer since. But in the longer term, we haven't seen much advance.

For 17-year-olds, for the past 10 years we really see no progress in terms of closing the achievement gap. Both groups, white students and black students, have pretty much been on a flat line during that period.

So the question is whether we're seeing younger students closing that gap and as they get older, the gap will continue to close when those children reach the 12th grade, or whether something happens to students that make them flat-line as they get into 10th, 11th, and 12th grade. I think we still have to wait a few years to know.

Importance of Leisure Reading

But let me introduce an important variable in understanding these scores and the achievement gap.

The American Enterprise Institute held a little symposium about 18 months ago that I attended. The speakers were leaders in areas of educational public policy, a few from the Department of Education and others from important think tanks such as the Fordham Foundation.

The interesting thing was, in terms of addressing the achievement gap, all of the discussion was about the classroom. All of the discussion was contained within the school setting. And the focus rested on different policies – school choice, different kinds of charter schools, looking at success stories such as KIPP schools, looking at some of the controversies over whole language instruction versus phonics instruction – but it was all understood within the school setting.

Now, the problem with this is that in the same NAEP report from which I took some of these scores, there were also numbers focusing upon leisure reading – the reading people do for fun. Not related to school, not having to do for work. And the correlation that comes up is, the more leisure reading you do, the higher your test scores. And it doesn't have to be serious literature. The more reading you do of comic books, romance novels – things totally unrelated to the work you're assigned – the higher your reading scores.

Furthermore, the test score differences between heavy and light fun readers exceed the differences between heavy and light in-class readers. The gap between the highest and next highest fun readers is 17 points, while the gap between the highest and next highest in-class readers is only four points. Likewise, the gap between the highest and lowest fun readers is 37 points, that between the highest and lowest in-class readers is 29 points.

Because the measurements of reading for school and reading for fun don't use the same scale (pages read vs. frequency of reading), we can't draw hard and fast conclusions about their respective effects on reading scores. But leisure reading does have some influence on school performance, much more than one would assume after listening to public and professional discourse about reading scores, which tends to focus on the classroom and the curriculum, not on the leisure lives of teens.

Blacks Lag in Leisure Reading

What is the significance of that? Consider a few more pieces of evidence about leisure reading.

The National Endowment of the Arts commissions large surveys of public participation in the arts, including the reading of books and literature.

When they look at 18- to 24-year-olds, they find large discrepancies in reading by non-Hispanic whites and non-Hispanic black young adults.

One question was whether the child read any fiction, poetry, or drama in the past 12 months. Forty-eight percent of non-Hispanic whites said yes. Only 34 percent of 18- to 24-year-old blacks said yes.

The final number I'll mention to you has to do with another survey that is done every year. It's called the American Freshman Survey, and it's conducted by a research institute at UCLA. It surveys about 250,000 freshmen in September. Recently, it found that black freshmen, those just entering college, actually do a little bit more leisure reading than do white freshmen. So, of the group going to college, you actually see it's almost equal, in terms of the leisure reading. This suggests that what people want to do with their non-school time might play a strong role in this achievement gap we're talking about.

A lot of the education community doesn't look at the leisure variable very closely. One has to ask how young people are spending the roughly five-and-a-half hours of leisure time they have each day. You've got an English teacher who has the students for about four hours a week, and they are lucky to get one to two hours of homework in that subject out of that student per week. That's about six hours total of in-class reading time.

The leisure time they have reaches about 45 hours per week. If in that leisure time reading is low, if you find leisure habits among young people that are not conducive at all to intellectual work, then all of the money going into the schools, the new reading programs that are being developed, the new strategies to inspire students in the classroom – they will have only a limited effect.

What we need to do is to look more at the non-school time, the non-school habitat, the type of literature in the home that the students return to, and see if the teachers can try to look at reading and reading achievement in a broader context of students' lives.

It's a heavy burden to place on the teachers, I know – but if we want to see progress, we have to get outside the classroom and look at the other institutions that support reading, such as public libraries, and see what kind of programs they develop.

Life-Changing Investment

Now, how does this relate to Booker T. Washington? This is a question, really, about how you understand your life. What do you want to do with your time? In school and in the workplace, you're largely told what to do. You have work assigned, you either do it well or you don't.

In your leisure time, you have peer pressure, and you have some home pressures, but there is a great deal more latitude in how you decide to spend your time. Boys have about six hours of leisure time per day, and girls have about five hours. What do you want to do with them? How do you want to fill that time?

It bears upon how you foresee your life. Where do you want to invest your own independence? Those minutes that you have on your own – do you want to spend them hanging out and talking on the cell phone, or do you want to watch TV, or do you want to spend 10 minutes a day reading a newspaper? Again, that's not much of an investment, but over time it might make a difference in how young people conceive of themselves as citizens.

Washington's work asks young people to look at their lives and make decisions about how they want to invest their time and energy – it certainly did for me when I first read *Up from Slavery*.

It's almost an economic conception of your leisure time, as well as your work time. What do you want to do to improve your knowledge, your understanding, your habits, your skills, and so on? This carries over well beyond the schoolroom, well beyond the workplace. It is an overall life transformation if you're going to really immerse yourself in Washington's vision.

In your leisure time, you decide what you want to do; you decide how you want to spend your time. You have so many minutes in the day, so many places to put your attention – and if you aren't wise about it, especially in a culture in which young people are bombarded with images and advertising and text messages and so on – if you aren't vigilant in the way you filter how you engage your energies, for class, for work, and in your leisure time, then you may sink.

This, I think, is where Washington's work ethic expands into a leisure ethic as well. It's not a matter of saying you can't read anything except the best. Any leisure reading, reading for fun, is good. Reading a newspaper, reading popular magazines – it's not a question of saying we want only high culture, we want only serious intellectual engagement. What we want is leisure activities that, at least for part of that leisure time, support the more serious intellectual and economic activities that one does engage in otherwise.

This is the lesson I take from Washington, and it is one I think the education system would benefit from paying more attention to.

Chapter 15

Washington and Rosenwald

Peter Ascoli, Ph.D.[17]

For Booker T. Washington, as for Julius Rosenwald – whom I call J.R. because his friends did – the key to solving some of the problems of race that plagued the United States in the early twentieth century was education. Before you could have entrepreneurship, which both men espoused – whether it be black entrepreneurship, which Washington championed, or white entrepreneurship, like Julius Rosenwald – you have to have children who can read and count. Hence, for both of them education was of paramount importance.

Julius Rosenwald was the CEO of Sears Rocbuck from 1908 to 1924. He never finished high school, and he never went to college – a fact that bothered him all his life. And yet he realized the centrality of education, and I think this was one of the things that greatly appealed to him about Booker T. Washington.

Although 1.9 percent of the population of Chicago was black in 1900, blacks really were not on Rosenwald's radar screen until 1910, when he was sent two books by a friend. One of them was *Up from Slavery*, which he read with great interest. The other was the biography of a Southern railroad magnate who was president of the General Education Board, one of the early Rockefeller philanthropies that dealt with education for both blacks and whites in the South.

Rosenwald was really struck by these books, and when he was visited shortly after reading them by a delegation from the YMCA of Chicago and was asked if he would be interested in putting up $25,000 to help build a black YMCA in Chicago, his immediate response was that he would give $25,000 to any YMCA in America that could raise an additional $75,000

---

[17] Dr. Peter Ascoli has been working on a biography of his grandfather, Julius Rosenwald, since 1993. Rosenwald is most famous for building Sears Roebuck, but he was also a philanthropist who generously supported Booker T. Washington's efforts.

to build a black Y. His interlocutors were astounded, and Rosenwald said modestly, "Well, maybe you can't build more than three a month, but I hope you can."

This began a program that resulted in the construction of 27 YMCAs in cities across America for black Americans. It's true these YMCAs were segregated, but in the Jim Crow era in which they were built, it was the only way they could be built.

They also served a purpose that was far above simply recreation, because they had dormitories. In Chicago, when African-Americans came to town looking for work and didn't have relatives to stay with, the only place they could go was a Y. So there was a real need for these YMCAs.

Meeting of Minds

As a result of his contributions to the YMCA, Rosenwald met Booker T. Washington in April 1911. It was suggested that Washington come and speak at a YMCA dinner. Rosenwald agreed to be the emcee, and although he had never met Washington, he agreed to host a luncheon of white business leaders to meet the famous Wizard of Tuskegee. The luncheon was successful, and Washington invited Rosenwald to serve on the board of Tuskegee. Rosenwald was unsure about that and said he wanted more time to think it over. In the meantime, he invited Washington and Dr. Hall, the famous physician, to visit him at the Sears plant.

This is interesting because Rosenwald was not immune to the prejudices of his day in that early period, and you can see how he changed from being quite racially prejudiced to being one of the more liberal thinkers of the early twentieth century. Right after he invited Washington to come to see him, Rosenwald wrote his wife and mentioned how the other employees of Sears were surprised to see these "Negras," as he called them. One sort of bridles at his use of that term, but shortly after this he would never use such expressions.

In any case, he and Washington got to know each other, and he visited Tuskegee and agreed to go on the board. He then invited Washington to stay at his home in Chicago, which would have been considered rather unusual in that era.

In 1912, for his 50th birthday, J.R. gave away $687,500 to a wide variety of organizations, and $25,000 of that went to Tuskegee. Specifically, it went to a program that he had talked about with Washington when Washington had stayed at his home.

There were quite a number of black private schools in the South, but many of them were in very poor financial condition. Rosenwald's idea was for a program that would be run by Washington, in which the money would be parceled out in small amounts as challenge grants and given to what we would call "capacity-building" to help them with fundraising, building needs, etc. Since Washington knew more about these schools than J.R. did, J.R. gave him the money and asked him to run the program.

Of course, Washington was delighted with this, but he had another agenda. That was to help build public schools in the area around Tuskegee. This idea was not original. He had interested another Tuskegee board member, a Standard Oil magnate who had agreed to put some money into building public schools but who died before the program could be implemented. Washington was eager to get this program started up again.

And so he asked Rosenwald if he could use one-tenth of the $25,000 in order to build five public schools in the area around Tuskegee. Rosenwald agreed to this, and in fact he agreed with alacrity. And initially he said, we can build these schools with Sears supplies, because Sears was already in the business of building homes. And Washington said no, that is not the point. The point is to have African-Americans help put up these schools and help pay for them.

Brilliant Fundraising
Washington was a brilliant fundraiser. He was extremely gifted, and he knew how to get people involved. And as the first five schools were built, he sent J.R. photographs of the construction work, and J.R. was captivated by them. J.R. would take trainloads of trustees from Chicago down to Tuskegee, and other trustees did this from other cities. This was a marvelous fundraising device.

In 1915, J.R. took a trainload of people down from Chicago, including Jane Addams and Chicago public schools superintendent Ella Flagg Young. There was quite a galaxy of people. Among other things, they visited some of these Rosenwald schools. J.R. was absolutely astonished.

Here were these spanking-new buildings – they were small, some of them only one room – but they really spruced up communities. They were supposed to double as not only schools but also as community centers. The other thing that really attracted J.R., which also had attracted him to the idea of the YMCAs, is that he saw this as a means of bringing the two races together. Working to build these schools, he thought, was a way of helping to bridge the race dilemma.

After J.R. saw these schools, Washington was easily able to persuade him to put more money into building more schools, and by the time of Washington's death in November 1915 some 85 schools had been started in three Southern states. They were called Rosenwald schools, and after Washington's death the program continued. Ultimately, more than 5,000 of these schools were built in 15 Southern states.

Need for Local Leadership

It's important to realize that you couldn't just build a school. Certain things were needed in the community in order to have one. You needed a spark, some person who was eager to work for and try to help found a school.

For example, there was a woman in one of these early communities where one of the first Rosenwald schools was built, Mary Johnson. She saw the terrible conditions under which the children in her town went to school, and she decided she was definitely going to change this. She got a group of women together, and they collected money, but they didn't have enough. Finally, they got the wood together, but she couldn't convince the men in the community to help put up the building. The wood rotted on the ground.

She tried again. They had bake sales, and finally they got enough money. Somebody absconded with it. And then a third time, again she went to work and raised the money. This time they put up most of the money, but she needed just the last bit – and this was where Rosenwald's money came in handy. She was able to put up the school. But if it hadn't been for Mary Johnson and others like her, it would have been difficult to build these schools in these communities.

This was a self-help movement. Rosenwald contributed only a quarter to a third of the money to put up the schools. The rest of the money came in sweat equity from local blacks, and some of it actually came from local whites, which is amazing when you consider this was the height of the Jim Crow era.

More than 50 percent of the money came from state and local government, and this was something that was possible only because of the recent developments of the General Education Board, this first Rockefeller charity, which had created state positions for black education. These were jobs that were held by whites, of course, but the whites who held them were really dedicated to the notion of assisting African-American education. They knew the ins and outs of government, and they were able to persuade state legislatures to put some money into black schools, something that had not occurred before. This was where the match was made that enabled Rosenwald schools to be built.

Agreement on Value of Education

By the time the program ended in 1932, 5,357 schools, shops, and teachers' homes had been built in 15 Southern states. Blacks put up a total of $4.7 million; state and local government paid 64 percent of the total, or $18.1 million; local whites put in $1.2 million; and J.R. actually put in less than the black total, $4.5 million.

I'd like to quote from the obituary W.E.B. DuBois wrote when Rosenwald died in 1932. DuBois said,

The death of Julius Rosenwald brings to an end a career remarkable especially for its significance to American Negroes. As a Jew, Julius Rosenwald did not have to be initiated into the methods of race prejudice, and his philanthropic work was a crushing arraignment of American white Christians. Knowing that the YMCA discriminated grossly against Negroes, Rosenwald calmly offered to help pay for Negro association building. To this end he gave large sums, and few people had the wit to smile at his slap in the face at white Christianity.

Seeing again that the white South did not propose to build decent schoolhouses for most colored children, Rosenwald again offered to help pay for such schoolhouses, provided they were real schoolhouses and on modern lines. The South accepted his gift effusively and never even to this day has apparently grasped the failure of democracy which permitted an individual of a despised race to do for the sovereign states of a great nation that which they had neither the decency nor justice to do for themselves.

Beyond this, Rosenwald reached out toward public libraries and hospitals and endowed a great fund to carry on his work after his death. He was a great man, but was no mere philanthropist. He was rather the subtle, stinging critic of our racial democracy.

The reason I quote this is that, as Professor Allen has said, I really think the division between DuBois and Washington has been overstated. I think both men would agree that primary schools that taught the three Rs as well as crafts were needed in America. I'm sure DuBois actually agreed with that, as has been said before. And therefore I believe the division between them, as has been noted at this conference before, has been vastly overstated.

PART 5

LEFT, RIGHT, AND BLACK

Chapter 16

Parting with Our Grievances

Ralph Conner[18]

The challenge we face today in the African-American community is to consider how Booker T. Washington's agenda is relevant from a political standpoint. I think not only African-Americans, but all Americans of good will, see something of value in Washington's program.

Was he a right-wing conservative? I don't think you could call him that. I don't think you should call me that, but many times I am called a right-wing conservative because I embrace a philosophy that does not depend on government. I embrace a philosophy that does not believe expansion of government services is what's best for mankind. I think individual liberty is what's best for mankind. Many people in academia will agree it's OK for a college kid to run amok, but they don't want a government that gives individual liberty to smokers or allows people to start their own businesses without over-regulation.

Booker T. Washington, were he with us today, would quickly recognize one of the key problems with many African-American leaders, which is their focus on past ills and grievances instead of solutions to the problems of today and tomorrow. I'd like to share with you a rather long quotation from Booker T. Washington on this topic. He wrote,

> Even before I had learned to read books or newspapers, I remember hearing my mother and other coloured people in our part of the country

---

[18] Ralph Conner is local legislation manager of The Heartland Institute and the former village president of Maywood, Illinois.

speak about Frederick Douglass's wonderful life and achievements. I heard so much about Douglass when I was a boy that one of the reasons why I wanted to go to school and learn to read was that I might read for myself what he had written and said. In fact, one of the first books that I remember reading was his own story of his life, which Mr. Douglass published under the title of "My Life and Times." This book made a deep impression upon me, and I read it many times.

Washington continues,

On one occasion, when I happened to be in Washington, I heard that Frederick Douglass was going to make a speech in a near-by town. I had never seen him nor heard him speak, so I took advantage of the opportunity. I was profoundly impressed by the man and by the address, but I did not dare approach even to shake hands with him. Some three or four years after I had organized Tuskegee Institute I invited Mr. Douglass to make a visit to the school and to speak at the commencement exercises of the school. He came and spoke to a great audience, many of whom had driven 30 or 40 miles to hear the great orator and leader of the race. In the course of time, I invited all of the prominent coloured men whose names I have mentioned, as well as others, to come to Tuskegee and speak to our students and to the coloured people in our community. ...

Mr. Douglass's great life-work had been in the political agitation that led to the destruction of slavery. He had been the great defender of the race, and in the struggle to win from Congress and from the country at large the recognition of the Negro's rights as a man and as a citizen he had played an important part. But the long and bitter political struggle in which he had engaged against slavery had not prepared Mr. Douglass to take up the equally difficult task of fitting the Negro for the opportunities and responsibilities of freedom. The same was true to a large extent of other Negro leaders. At the time when I met these men and heard them speak I was invariably impressed, though young and inexperienced, that there was something lacking in their public utterances. I felt that the millions of Negroes needed something more than to be reminded of their suffering and of their political rights; that they needed to do something more than merely to defend themselves. ...

I remember one young man in particular who graduated from Yale University and afterward took a postgraduate course at Harvard, and who began his career by delivering a series of lectures on "The Mistakes of Booker T. Washington." It was not long, however, before he found that he could not live continuously on my mistakes. Then he discovered that in all his long schooling he had not fitted himself to perform any kind of useful and productive labour. After he had failed in several other directions he appealed to me, and I tried to find something for him to do. It is pretty hard, however, to help a young man who has started wrong. Once he gets the idea that – because he has crammed his head full with mere book knowledge – the world owes him a living, it is hard for him to change. The last I heard of the young man in question, he was trying to eke out a miserable existence as a book agent while he was looking about for a position somewhere with the Government as a janitor or for some other equally humble occupation. ...

A story told me by a coloured man in South Carolina will illustrate how people sometimes get into situations where they do not like to part with their grievances. In a certain community there was a coloured doctor of the old school, who knew little about modern ideas of medicine, but who in some way had gained the confidence of the people and had made considerable money by his own peculiar methods of treatment. In this community there was an old lady who happened to be pretty well provided with this world's goods and who thought that she had a cancer. For twenty years she had enjoyed the luxury of having this old doctor treat her for that cancer. As the old doctor became – thanks to the cancer and thanks to other practice – pretty well-to-do, he decided to send one of his boys to a medical college. After graduating from the medical school, the young man returned home, and his father took a vacation. During this time the old lady who was afflicted with the "cancer" called in the young man, who treated her; within a few weeks, the cancer (or what was supposed to be the cancer) disappeared, and the old lady declared herself well.

When the father of the boy returned and found the patient on her feet and perfectly well, he was outraged. He called the young man before him and said: "My son, I find that you have cured that cancer case of mine. Now, son, let me tell you something. I educated you on that cancer. I put you through high school, through college, and finally through the medical school on that cancer. And now you, with your new ideas of practising medicine, have come here and cured that cancer. Let me tell you, son, you have started all wrong. How do you expect to make a living practising medicine in that way?"

Is someone a "conservative" because he points out what is missing from the speeches and agendas of those who rely on government exclusively to advance the black community? I don't think so.

Ladies and gentlemen, I think it's important that we understand that as a storyteller, political cynic, author, leader, thought-setter, and progressive humanitarian, Booker T. Washington ranks high above the men of his generation. His ideas certainly are worthy of our attention today.

Chapter 17

Need for a Wider Audience

Carol M. Swain, Ph.D.[19]

We have much work to do if we are to bridge the current racial and political divide in America.

One of the most urgent things we need to do is create situations where honest dialogue can take place among people who ordinarily avoid one another. The most critical problems impacting our nation and African-Americans in particular will not be solved by like-minded people conversing with one another.

A Dysfunctional Community

Right, left, middle – where should blacks go politically? We first have to critique ourselves as a people. If Booker T. Washington were alive today and he saw the situation of African-Americans, I believe he would be in deep despair because even though there has been much progress, such as the expansion of the black middle-class, there remain parts of the community that are totally dysfunctional by mainstream standards. What we are doing as a community is simply not working. We are in need of hope and healing. Our good news is tempered by bad news.

Look at the unacceptably high rates of incarceration, drug abuse, illegitimacy, unwed motherhood, and abortion. Although the black teenage birth rate is down, it is not because people are not having sex and getting pregnant – it is down because so many of our teenagers are aborting their babies. Where is Jesse Jackson when you need him? Why is he not decrying the loss of millions of potential black voters? Where's the black political left on this issue of abortion? Why are they not talking about this issue when so many black babies are being aborted? Where are the voices of denunciation?

---

[19] Dr. Carol M. Swain is professor of political science and professor of law at Vanderbilt University.

This is a critical issue that should concern all of us. We talk about sterilization, we talk about genocide, we talk about all these things that are happening in black communities, but we are not talking about the abortion clinics. We are not talking about the fact that our churches are not adequately addressing this issue. I think if Booker T. Washington were alive today, he would be decrying this situation and he would say, "Black America, have you lost your mind?"

Lack of Political Coherence

We have many white friends in the conservative movement. We cannot count on all of them to share our concerns. Conservative is a broad label, and it includes people who are well-meaning as well as those who do not care about black folks. These conservatives do not care about abortion or about hopelessness and despair. They may like part of what Booker T. Washington had to say but they are not willing to go all the way with his prescription – because if they went all the way they would be forced to take a different position on immigration and some of the other issues negatively impacting black communities.

The same is true of their attitudes toward Martin Luther King Jr. These conservatives hear what they want to hear. We have a long way to go before we get to the point where we can have truly viable multiracial coalitions. Glenn Loury talked about black issues being an American problem. I agree that many of them are American problems, because we are all Americans, but there are some things only African-Americans can do for themselves. We must set our own high standards of morality and justice and do a better job of internally policing our communities.

We suffer from negative stereotypes. Unfortunately, every negative stereotype has a grain of truth. Once black Americans change persistent negative behavioral patterns, negative stereotypes will also change. As we change our self-image as a group, more people of other races and ethnicities will be willing to join forces with us to fight for the betterment of society.

Need for Biblical Principles

Where should blacks go politically? One thing is for sure: The problems decimating our communities are so intractable they are not likely to be solved simply by using man-made political solutions. As a person of faith and as a believer in the principles taught by Jesus Christ and by the Christian Bible, I do not and can not believe that man has the solution to all of his problems. For African-Americans to make real racial and political progress, we need to return to the spiritual principles and precepts that teach us how to live as moral human beings. We must say no to the choices that lead to death and dysfunctional lifestyles.

Today we are celebrating Booker T. Washington, and we are quoting him, but we often leave aside the point that he was a deeply religious man, and that a great deal of his wisdom came from Biblical principles. Somehow we must get black people to stop talking about religion and begin living by those moral principles that significantly improve the quality of one's life.

If Booker T. Washington were alive today, I believe he would be pressing African-Americans to return to conservative moral principles about right living. He would urge the men to take care of their families. Welfare reform was great and it has been very successful. I come from a family where there have been many people on welfare for years. Now many of them have jobs – they are dead-end jobs, but nevertheless they have jobs.

We need to go to the next step. Many of the same people who endorsed welfare reform support churches getting welfare. They do this by supporting the faith-based initiatives of the Bush administration. That is essentially giving welfare to churches. Often, the money constrains what religious leaders can talk about from the pulpit. If welfare is not good for individuals, it is certainly not good for churches.

Need to Deracialize Issues

Many of the problems that are affecting African-Americans need to be deracialized. Some issues are particular to the black community, but others are not really about race. Take felony disenfranchisement, for example. We have made it a racial issue. But I think it is framed wrong. A more strategic way to frame that issue would be to argue that when any person has paid his or her debt to society, it is unjust to continue to exact a punishment once the sentence is served. The issue is not about race, because felony disenfranchisement affects every convicted felon, differently depending on the laws of a given state. More people would support the repeal of felony disenfranchisement laws if the issue were not framed as being one that primarily affects black men.

There are many such issues that disproportionately impact African-Americans that are not about race. We talk about the disparity in punishment for crack cocaine offenders and cocaine offenders, and we say it is all about race, but it was actually black leaders who pushed for stiffer penalties because of the impact crack was having in their communities. This is a conveniently forgotten fact.

We have responsibilities to do more than just talk about the problems. We have to be willing to go into the inner city and get our hands dirty. We can become role models for the young people who cross our paths. But we also have to tell them that role models don't always have to look like you. Role models do not have to be of the same race or gender to motivate a person to try harder. Most of my early role models were white men. If role models had to look like those they motivate, there would never be any "firsts."

Need to Reach Out

The most important thought I would like to leave you with is our need to reach out to more people. We are reaching out, but somehow we have to get more people to the point where they feel comfortable engaging in a dialogue on the issues of race. No one political side has all the answers.

The problems of African-Americans will not be solved by politics or by black people working alone. We need others working alongside us to change our culture. We also need fresh ideas and new ways of attacking perennial problems.

We have to take the lead. No matter how caring and well-meaning a person is from another racial or ethnic group, I do not believe they are going to have the depth of concern or trust that a member of the same group will elicit. We can enlist whites as allies, but at the end of the day it's our responsibility to find solutions to the problems decimating black communities. And whether we like it or not, human beings are tribal. Birds of a feather do stick together, and God has wired us in such a way that we lean towards members of our own groups first. That does not have to always be negative.

Black people have a greater responsibility to reach out to other blacks in trouble. No one's going to love little black males the way we should love them. In their faces, we see our children, and we smile at our children. We love our children and we have to do more to help save them.

Indeed, these are life and death issues that are getting lost in the debate. We need to think separately about each of these different issues decimating black communities. Every issue that can be deracialized, should be deracialized. It is a matter of practical politics.

Chapter 18

Progress and Disappointments

William B. Allen, Ph.D.[20]

I've never been a very modest man, but I am humble and grateful to have been invited to participate in this conference by one of the conveners of the famous Fairmont Conference in 1980.

That was an occasion on which a number of black thinkers and practitioners, about the time of the election of President Ronald Reagan, were assembled at the Fairmont Hotel in San Francisco to ask the same question we are being asked to consider. And I look at that, and the association between the two, and I think, surely we are not expected to reproduce what Thomas Sowell and Lee Walker and Hank Lucas and so many others did in 1980 at that moment of opportunity, as they saw it then at the Fairmont Hotel.

For everyone expected that with the advent of the Reagan administration there would not only come into power in the United States a new conservative focus but also a new opportunity to phrase the issue of the status of American blacks in a way that was finally compatible with the promise of American constitutionalism. So it was an exciting moment. I heard about it almost as soon as it took place and was much informed of the hopefulness that came out of that conference.

So we stand now 26 years later and ask the question, "What became of that hopefulness?"

In some respects, many wonderful things happened. Many wonderful careers blossomed in the aftermath of that conference, and it produced much of value, not only to the discussion about American blacks, but to the United States itself.

On the other hand, some things have happened since that time that surely must have been disappointments to those who were present at the Fairmont Hotel. They must truly have concluded that progress was not all

---

[20] Dr. William B. Allen is professor of political science at Michigan State University.

they had hoped for. And they would have liked to have seen this conversation eventuate in somewhat more strongly establishing a consensus about the centrality of the experience of American blacks in our understanding of the nature of American constitutionalism.

Two Failures

Certainly that's the only way to talk about Booker T. Washington ultimately and meaningfully. To see him as someone who has contributed, in the mode of our greatest constitutional thinkers, in trying to give shape and meaning to the expression of the American dream. Not trying to describe what it means to be black, even while being intensely focused upon strategically situating freed slaves so as to participate fully in that dream.

Now some of the things that made it difficult for all of the hoped-for progress to take place are well-known to us today. There were two important failures. One was Martin Luther King's failure, and the other was Richard Nixon's. We are continuing to struggle with those two failures, which hung like a great shadow over the Fairmont Conference and everything else that has transpired since that time.

Martin Luther King's failure was this: In the vast statement of his project, the book *Where Do We Go From Here. Chaos or Community*, for the foundation of his mission he turned not to the promise of America but to the grievances of blacks. He makes the literal statement in that book that having suffered as we have suffered – having become victims – no one can expect us to stand on our own. Thus the dialog has to be, "What is the government going to do to overcome our victimization?" That was the last thing Martin Luther King gave us, whereas earlier he had pointed us toward fulfillment in the American dream.

Rhetoric of Victimhood

That failure is the reason the rhetoric within the American black community today cannot rise above victimhood. Now, I do not mean to depreciate King's stature. The reason I mention his failure is because he was a great man, he was the only American in the twentieth century to attain the stature of George Washington and Abraham Lincoln. That's how great he was.

But when you see how great he was, you know also how great was the opportunity he had, and which he spurned, when he took that wrong turn and left us to continue to struggle bootlessly, talking about grievances, when what the hour called for was what the Fairmont Conference hoped for: proactive, positive, creative engagement calling forth the greatest strength and the enormous resilience our prior history had given such evidence of, and nowhere so profoundly as in the life of Booker T. Washington.

On the first night of this conference, Bobbie Johnson spoke about Booker T. and 50 Cents. And just to show you what the status of our discourse is, for a moment I was ready to erupt in appreciation that someone in the country besides me remembered that in 1949 and 1950 there was a half-dollar coin in circulation honoring Booker T. Washington. And George Washington Carver, yes! I have them; I've collected them myself. That's what I thought she was talking about, only to be disappointed to learn she was talking about some contemporary rap performer.

You see, I'm trying to recover the nobler, the grander vision, without getting lost in the tawdriness of some of the contemporary things we're focused on. It means remembering that the country once recognized how great Booker T. Washington was. The national currency proclaimed it to us! The reverse of the coin said, "United in Brotherhood." And it meant everybody!

The dream of American constitutional existence stands at the center of the dialog about left and right, liberal and conservative, and this is where Nixon comes into the story.

Politics of Victimhood

Richard Nixon said he was a Tory who would govern by liberal principles. He said it, and he meant it. He's the man who gave us racial preferences. He's the one who converted affirmative action into the strong instrument of race-based decision-making with which we struggle to this very day and have not escaped. It is because he bound upon the country affirmative action preferences that he wedded the victim mentality, the welfare state mentality, with the affirmative action mentality to give us affirmative action welfare. And we have not yet escaped it. It was a terrible, terrible failure.

Its architects have all confessed their error. Larry Silberman said it was a mistake; we shouldn't have done it; we didn't know what we were doing. The important thing to remember, though, is that it happened because it was allowed by someone who stood in the position to have prevented it: Richard Nixon and his attorney general could have said no, and that would have been the end of it. It would not have happened. It was not that it was being clamored for in a great public way by the opposition. But it was a clever strategy, and often liberalism-conservatism reduces to just that: clever strategies, where people don't take into account the ultimate constitutional consequences of these clever strategies.

So I listened to Ishmael Muhammad refuse to consider himself an American, declaring himself a human being instead, and therefore also refusing to embrace the promise of American constitutionalism. And I see exactly where we are now; I see exactly what the options are and where we need to go. For it is clearly the refusal to embrace the promise of American constitutionalism that is the enormous threat that hangs over our discourse. We are nothing better than what America promises to become.

Discourse of Victimhood

The big question to ask is: How did we get to be human beings? What did Ishmael Muhammad mean? It rolls off the tongue so easily: "I'm a human." But as Dr. Swain has just made clear to us, there are some aspects of tribalism that are appealing to people, always have been. And I will tell you, the tribal perspective is the native perspective. The human perspective is not native.

I'm not going to say now how this idea of humanity was invented. I may not get to do that today, because that must be done in the proper context. But I will tell you it is the most important question for which no one before has had the answer. And that gets in the way of trying to explain what we're going to do about the race question, because it is strictly subordinate to the human question.

But we have a shortcut. Since we can't answer the big question, we can approach it by way of certain smaller questions. The smaller question is this: What is America all about? And the way to phrase that is to say what we care about is to be able to articulate an understanding of America that embraces our best hopes for all persons in the country. That should be our standard.

We can talk about poverty. I do not oppose people expressing concern about poverty, but I ask them to remember what I've said previously: Wealth is infinite! There is no limitation. There is nothing that prevents anyone from becoming wealthy, because wealth is created by human beings. And the endless tides of immigrants who come over and establish wealth for themselves prove it time and again. Nothing stands in the way of anyone becoming wealthy; no government program is needed to accomplish it.

Overcoming Victimhood

And so to summarize the real thrust of these particular observations, I will say that I too have had a Booker T. Washington moment. I'm not a Washington scholar, but I've had a Booker T. Washington moment.

It occurred in 1981, shortly after the Reagan administration had come into power. There was assembled in the Lincoln Room, if I recall, a meeting of something called the Council for a Black Economic Agenda. We met there with the president, the vice president, and numerous cabinet officials. It was an intense and powerful moment.

When the conference was over, and we all had dispersed to our respective locations, I carried with me a brooding sense that something had gone wrong. And I went home and sat down and penned an op-ed to describe what I thought had gone wrong. The title to this op-ed was, "Mr. President, Can You Lend Me a Dime?"

That was my Booker T. Washington moment, when I saw that even supposedly conservative American blacks at this moment of power, this opportunity for influence, were too narrowly focused on marginal improvements in their respective circumstances. Looking for a handout, not offering a hand to someone else *to* help, but extending a hand *for* help.

That's my Booker T. Washington moment. Washington wanted no descendant of the slaves ever to be in the position of asking anyone, anywhere for help. He wanted them always to be in the position of offering to help everyone, in everything. He wanted them always to want to credential themselves sufficiently that people would have to look to them for help. Booker T. Washington wanted to slay modesty.

We see the evidence for this in an indirect way in a book written by William F. Buckley in the late 1950s and early 1960s. The book is titled *Up from Liberalism*. Booker T. Washington is never mentioned in the book. Quite obviously the title is borrowed from *Up from Slavery*. One of the ways to understand the political opportunities, the political options before us, is to try to figure out how Booker T. Washington became the inspiration for William F. Buckley.

Chapter 19

Models of Success

Frank Harold Wilson, Ph.D.[21]

I am a sociologist who uses a historical perspective to analyze problems of changing social structure, race relations, and biography.

In appreciating the historical perspective, the principle of sankofa, which comes from Ghana in West Africa, is appropriate. Sankofa is symbolized by a bird that is looking backward and forward. This underscores that in order to go forward, we need to be informed by the past. History identifies for us models of success that should be drawn from, as well as examples of past mistakes that should be avoided.

In approaching this question, I am compelled to draw from the insights and example of Booker T. Washington. Washington's ideas in *Up from Slavery* indicate a critical (if not cautious) view of politics and voting; something that should occur after economic freedom had occurred. Office-holding, voting, and politics among blacks contradicted the goals of useful education, entrepreneurship, and land ownership.

This appears to be more of the public Washington. In practice, Washington was not totally against politics or social action. Throughout his life, he played both sides of the "political fence" when it came to getting support and resources for Tuskegee. As far as national politics, Washington was a Republican who was well-aligned with Republican presidents. When it came to state and local politics, Washington knew he had to deal and negotiate with Democrats.

The question of where to go in the political arena is both a "burning question" and a proposal for action. In addressing this issue (or set of issues), I will discuss the following. First, what is meant by left and right – traditionally and contemporaneously? Second, I will examine some of the possibilities of black Americans with respect to the left-right divide in the twenty-first century.

---

[21] Dr. Frank Harold Wilson is associate professor of sociology at the University of Wisconsin at Milwaukee.

Defining Left and Right

The terms left and right have political, economic, and social significance. Usually when these terms are discussed they are limited to the political context. Left (or leftist) centers on individuals or political groups advocating liberal, radical, or revolutionary political programs, an expanded role of democratic governments, and the empowering of the masses. During the twentieth century, the left has included "welfare-statists," democratic socialists, Marxian socialists, communists, and anarchists. Right (or rightist) centers on individuals or political groups advocating conservative or reactionary political programs, a restricted role of democratic governments (restrictions on the power of the masses), and oligarchical rule. During the twentieth century, the right has included conservatives, neoconservatives, libertarians, the American independent party, the John Birch Society, the Ku Klux Klan, and the American Nazi party. Traditionally, most rightists regarded themselves as "moderates" or "middle of the roaders." Since the 1980s, a Christian Coalition called the Moral Majority has redefined the boundaries of the right.

The terms left and right also have an economic dimension, which focuses on how capitalism should grow (which is usually allied with the political parties but not necessarily). New Deal liberal economics, in response to the Great Depression of the 1930s, came to embrace principles of interventionist government, macroeconomics, pragmatic experimentation, and federal government centralization. Keynesian economics were accompanied by the welfare state, economic redistribution policies, and civil rights. During recent decades, neoliberal economics have urged a model of economic growth that is derived from new investments in appropriate technology, entrepreneurship, military reform, human capital, national service, and industrial innovation.

Conservative economics have come to embrace growth through "trickle down" economics, deregulation, short-term profits through intermediary enterprises, and the devolution of federal government functions to the states and local governments. Conservative economic policies, which were spurred on by the Reagan Revolution, were accompanied by corporate restructuring and mergers, reindustrialization, and outsourcing. Although conservative economics were traditionally focused on the production of necessary goods and services, in the contemporary economy this is less clear. Conservatives invoke discourses of laissez-faire capitalism (although this has long been replaced for the most part).

Contemporary Left and Right

Where are the left and right in contemporary American politics, and how does this compare with the historic left and right in American politics?

The political landscape in terms of left and right has changed considerably in comparison with the post-World War II and Cold War years. The political left was influenced in part by larger international politics (and propaganda wars) and domestic politics. The challenges of communism and socialism abroad; struggles for national liberation and independence in Africa, Asia, Latin America, and other Southern Hemisphere nations; movements such as the workers movement and Civil Rights movement; and various localized struggles for community empowerment broadened the definition of rights and access.

Since the late 1980s, the contemporary left has had less of the international communism in the USSR, East Germany, and Eastern Europe to define its agenda. The "springtime" of freedom in the developing Third World has been accompanied by the "winter" challenges of nation-building, economic growth, political stability, and indebtedness. As a consequence of declining membership, compromises in collective bargaining, and increasingly being unable to strike, organized labor (or labor unions) represents a much smaller part of labor (and particularly industrial labor organizations). The United States has one of the proportionately smallest organized labor sectors among advanced industrial nations. The more "radical flank" of Civil Rights movement organizations of the 1960s (SNCC and CORE) are nearly nonexistent. Movement organizations such as the NAACP remain focused on promoting integration and protecting existing civil rights policies.

The contemporary liberal-left is increasingly defined by a diversity of groups that pursue race, gender, lifestyle, environmental, and identity politics. The Rainbow Coalition during the 1980s and the Green Party during the 1990s have represented the radical flanks. Unions organized around professional and government workers, rather than industrial unions, represent the largest. The rise and establishment of the women's movement in Democratic Party politics has been important. Status and identity politics, focused on issues such as comparable worth, homosexuals in the military, and same-sex marriages, have also been prominent.

The contemporary conservative-right has a coalition between corporate and business groups, conservative foundations, conservative PACs and movements, and "middle" Americans. Most businesses are on the political right.

Black Americans and the Left-Right Divide
Black Americans, in terms of political party affiliation, have been characterized by two dominant patterns from Reconstruction to the present. From Reconstruction to the first Franklin D. Roosevelt administration, black Americans were overwhelmingly affiliated with the Republican Party (although it should be kept in context that most black Americans were either disenfranchised or marginalized). Since 1936, black Americans have largely shifted to the Democratic Party.

However, black American representation in the Republican Party was more substantial during the early post-World War II years (including the Eisenhower administration). The Goldwater, Nixon, and Reagan political strategies involved a stronger "Southern strategy" that was distanced from black American voters. Since the Voting Rights Act of 1965, black Americans have been heavily represented in the Democratic Party (typically 90 percent).

Differing Pictures of Discrimination

The most important concern identified by black Americans in social research and public opinion has not changed since early in the twentieth century. Economic access to jobs, business loans, mortgages, and credit were identified in Gunnar Myrdal's *An American Dilemma* (1944) and more recent public opinion surveys. Political access has followed economic access (and is usually viewed as necessary). Among business, political, religious, and civil rights leaders, there has been consensus around the importance of economics as the principal strategy. There have been different approaches.

During recent decades, there has been a changing mood with respect to racial attitudes among white Americans. During the 1960s and 1970s, white Americans were more likely to view the racial inequality experienced by black Americans as substantially influenced by structural causes, including discrimination. Since the 1980s, the racial inequality experienced by black Americans is much more likely to be interpreted by white Americans in terms of individualistic causes (that resonate with the changing political and cultural discourses). The causes for black inequality are perceived as connected with blacks not working hard enough rather than structural discrimination.

Black Americans have consistently identified discrimination and prejudice more frequently than white Americans in public opinion surveys. The objective facts tell a different story. Structural economic barriers persist with respect to black employment, income, and occupational mobility. Housing discrimination through redlining and steering continues to exist independent of black American income levels.

And there are more elaborate and complex forms of contemporary discrimination. Research by Devah Pager found that white ex-felons received more calls from employers than blacks who did not have prison records. Related studies indicate employers may screen prospective employees on the basis of first and last names.

There are few signs that the "color line" and racism in America will disappear in the twenty-first century. Booker T. Washington would view these contemporary conditions as warranting greater self-reliance among black Americans.

Possibilities for Changing Politics

What are the possibilities of black Americans remaining a large part of the liberal-Democratic coalition in the twenty-first century? Are the changing social and economic conditions among black Americans that intersect with political action leaning in the direction of their remaining 85 to 90 percent in the Democratic Party?

By contrast, what are the possibilities of recent conservative initiatives in attracting black Americans to the Republican Party and conservative right? Highly visible appointments such as Clarence Thomas to the U.S. Supreme Court and Condoleezza Rice and Colin Powell as secretaries of state symbolize new aspirations of black Americans in the party.

During recent decades, the Republican Party has attempted to attract black voters, make inroads into black community leadership, and influence black public opinion. Milwaukee, where I have lived for the past 18 years, has been a social laboratory for conservative initiatives such as school choice, faith-based initiatives, enterprise and community empowerment zones, and the like. I sense that a primary part of this attraction will center on "bread and butter" economic issues and a secondary part will focus on moral conservatism.

Political attitude surveys done by Robert Smith and Richard Seltzer in *Race, Class, and Culture* have explored the relationship between black Americans remaining politically and economically liberal but more morally conservative. Politically and economically liberal attitudes are clearly connected with redistribution policies and civil rights and cut across all social classes among black Americans. At the same time, Smith and Seltzer note that compared to white Americans, black Americans are less interested in politics, less knowledgeable about politics, less trusting of government, and more alienated (Smith and Seltzer, 1993; pp. 43-44).

Blacks were alienated (less trusting or willing to work with others) due to their position in the racist class structure. Although blacks in the lower class had higher alienation rates than middle-class blacks, middle-class blacks were found to have higher alienation rates than lower-class whites (Smith and Seltzer, 1993).

Black Americans' Moral Conservatism

The moral conservatism among black Americans is derived from their proportionately larger affiliation and participation in church, which also has implications for more fundamentalist interpretations of social issues. Although dimensions of moral conservatism cut across black Americans, it usually runs higher among less-educated persons. Based on responses to the General Social Survey, black Americans indicated high moral conservatism in their attitudes toward homosexuality (92 percent to 76 percent say it is always wrong; less than high school and college graduates, respectively, and their disapproval of the ban on prayer in schools (84% to

71%; less than high school and college graduates, respectively), anti-communist views (consistently 70 percent and greater across social classes), extramarital sex (75% to 61.9% always wrong; less than high school and college graduates respectively), and abortion (60% to 41% always wrong; less than high school and college graduates respectively).

Conservatism among blacks was weakest in the non-South (42.6) and the largest 1-12 Standard Metropolitan Statistical Areas (41.1 – least conservative). It was stronger in the South (47.9), other urban (49.3), and rural communities.

The recent growth of black mega-churches, in contrast to older mega-churches, has taken place in outlying and suburban areas away from inner-city neighborhoods. These churches are particularly strong in the South, to which black migrants are increasingly returning. It appears that most of these churches are nondenominational, which gives them much flexibility. It remains to be seen whether agendas such as the "Black Contract with America on Moral Values" that have been initiated by leading black televangelists will translate politically.

There is already a discussion taking place within black America that is refocusing attention on black Americans again taking the moral agency and responsibility for their lives, relationships, families, and communities. Black Americans are again being challenged to empower themselves educationally and economically "from the ground up." With health crises such as HIV/AIDS, black Americans are being challenged to define their relationships and families more righteously and spiritually.

Challenge to Conserve

In the twenty-first century, black Americans will again be challenged to conserve and save more and waste less. There are lessons from our own history and international examples to inform this. Character and substance, rather than the superficial and the theatrical, will be emphasized.

The focus on consumption and "conspicuous consumption" by black Americans reached new heights during the post-civil rights era. The mindless energy and hours spent on conspicuous consumption and escapism can instead be focused on useful education, entrepreneurship, social relationships, and family.

There are several structural issues that will continue to cut across the left-right divide. These are bipartisan issues on which neither the Democrats nor Republicans have a monopoly.

1. Changes in education and higher education are needed, to emphasize high levels of mathematics, science, literacy, and computer literacy. The focus will also center on connecting school-to-work transitions and decreasing "special education" (which has been a dumping ground for black boys). Students should be alerted that they have to work smarter and harder and must endure to the end.

2. Entrepreneurship should be encouraged, emphasizing greater business cooperation and organization-building across family and metropolitan boundaries. Youth entrepreneurial programs need to be encouraged. African-American Chambers of Commerce, historically black colleges and universities, and historically white colleges and universities can articulate mentorship and bridge programs.

3. Home ownership should be encouraged as much as possible through federal and private programs. This is a win-win situation for local economies, communities, and citizens. During the 1990s there were the highest gains in black American home ownership, although the equity was at much lower levels.

4. Prison reform is essential. The sentencing disparities in terms of crack cocaine relative to pure cocaine accompanied "get tough on crime" policies. These have almost eliminated probation and parole and increased the chances of imprisonment.

5. The continuing "color line" must be addressed. With respect to addressing the institutional barriers of race, Booker T. Washington would have recognized that various strategies of policy, many universal and others race-specific, as practical matters will continue to be advocated in the twenty-first century. These should be secondary to the education and entrepreneurship objectives.

Washington's Challenge

Washington would be disappointed, but not detoured, by the continuing denials, rationalizations, and arrogance around racism and race in America. He would probably challenge black Americans to make a U-turn from much of what took place during the civil rights and post-civil rights years. As a "man of action" he left us a legacy of institution- and organization-building, "bridge building" across the racial divide, and race pride. While bipartisan and practical politics must increasingly be considered, his ideas on economics, education, and self-reliance are the ideas we are required to come back to and build on.

Over and over again, he reminds us of the possibilities of struggles and success. In his biography, *Up from Slavery*, Washington shares the wisdom:

I have learned that success is to be measured not so much by the position one has reached in life as by the obstacles which he has overcome while trying to succeed. With few exceptions, the Negro youth must work harder and perform his tasks even better than a white youth in order to secure recognition. But out of the hard and unusual struggle through which he is compelled to pass, he gets a strength, a confidence, that one misses whose pathway is smooth by reason of birth and race. (Washington, 1901; 27)

PART 6

SELF-RELIANCE AND THE ROLE OF GOVERNMENT

Chapter 20

The Need for Intellectual Diversity

Daryl Scott, Ph.D.[22]

When Lee Walker asked me to speak about Booker T. Washington, I knew this was part of a debate that I had had with him some 24 years ago when we first met. At that time I was not as high on Booker T. as I am today.

For the past four years I've devoted my time to rebuilding what was previously called the Association for the Study of Negro Life and History, and what is now the Association for the Study of African-American Life and History, founded by Carter G. Woodson. In doing so I've had to learn a lot about the business of the association over the years – it was a mess.

Woodson, as I learned, was an independent in many ways, but the association was founded by people who were stark Washingtonians – they were not DuBoisians. The first president of the association was Cleveland Hall, who was Washington's personal physician. The second president of the association was Robert E. Park. Most of you may know him as the father of the Chicago school of sociology, but you true students of Booker T. Washington know him as Washington's white personal secretary. He was a white man, who in the South would serve a black man. A very interesting guy. Another president of the association was Mary McLeod Bethune, a coworker with Booker T. Washington in the South, uplifting blacks through education.

---

[22] Dr. Daryl Scott is professor of history and chairman of the History Department at Howard University.

I think it's important to understand that the traditions merged together in the association. Now most folks in the association think of themselves as DuBoisian, and I always have to bring them back. I want to invite those of you who are true conservatives to join the association. It should be a very big tent; it has a tradition of being where African-Americans and people of all perspectives can play.

Don't let any one group of people decide the intellectual discourse. I want to urge everyone to participate – we need a debate from the left and from the right in the black community. That has been my perspective all my career. Most of the time in the academy I'm considered a member of the right – and gee, that just shows how left they can be!

Revenge of the Intellectuals

If Booker T. Washington was concerned about his historical image, it is very good that he wrote an autobiography. It has been virtually the only widely accessible testimony on his behalf. Over time, he lost his debate with DuBois, and as the victors the DuBoisians of the academic world are the keepers of African-American memory and the purveyors of black culture in mainstream America. Washington often poked fun at the intellectual pretensions of the black elite, so we should not be surprised that more than a few black intellectuals have made their careers denigrating him. It is in fact the easiest and most reliable cheap shot in the arsenal of most liberal and black intellectuals.

The political scientist Adolph Reed, to name one prominent example, knows he can successfully heap derision on virtually any opponent by likening him to Booker T. Washington. Washington cannot find a biographer who champions his views, or even treats them fairly or sympathetically, because DuBois's influence has been pervasive even among serious historians, as Robert Norrell has pointed out. I think we're going to have to wait until Robert writes his biography to have any chance of having a balanced view of Booker T. Washington.

As a profession, we historians have failed you, because if the liberal left has created this body of biased literature against Washington, you have been left with nothing but Washington's writings, and in reading his writings, quite often out of context, you have created a Washington that's not to my mind a historical Washington either.

While professionally my research has never focused on Washington, I have been reading his writings for nearly 40 years, beginning in grammar school. As a scholar I have spent a great deal of time doing intellectual history and thinking about the context in which Washington operated. In particular, I have been working on a history of white nationalism in the American South. If Washington has been misunderstood, so has the general history of race relations in the South. (I'm going to exclude Robert

Norrell's book, which I haven't had a chance to read. Apparently he has it right, so there may be some change in that.)

Southern White Nationalism

If scholars have had to cut through the work of liberal historians to find the real Booker T. Washington, the history of white nationalism in the American South is a lost world. It is lost to those very same scholars, and lost to American scholars in general. Whereas black nationalism is espied everywhere in the South, even where it didn't exist, white nationalism is seen nowhere.

This, too, is part of liberal denial, but it is a denial from which conservatives suffer as well. To see a past people with white nationalism is to call into question a cherished belief of liberals and modern conservatives alike – that America is and always has been an idea, and if only you throw up your right hand and espouse the creed, you are an American.

If this had been true, neither DuBois nor Washington would have had a project. What I'm arguing is that liberals want to say that there's racism, but that apart from this racism the creed is in place. Some sorts of discrimination are so fundamental they leave you outside the political community, and if you are outside the political community, you are not part of the nation. And in any nation that so circumscribes itself on that basis, on the basis of race, you have a racial nationalism. And a racial nationalism has been alive and well in America, particularly in the American South.

It should go without saying that Booker T. Washington was a product of his times, but the trick, as always, is to figure out the times and to fit the man in them. When one does this, it reveals the limits of what our contemporaries, liberal or conservative, have tried to make of Washington. In the context of his times, Washington was liberal, not conservative. His beliefs on race relations, black identity, racial uplift, the proper role of philanthropy, and the ideal state put him at odds with conservatives of his day and, I suggest to you, at odds with conservatives of today.

In today's political vocabulary, the ideals of self-reliance and self-help are the tell-tale signs of conservatism. Among liberal and conservative commentators on race relations, self-help sets apart conservatives from liberals. The often unspoken assumption is that liberals believe the state should solve the economic problems of the poor, and conservatives believe the individual should be self-reliant, that social welfare policies always engender dependency.

Working with this modern binary of state help versus self-help, the historian Wilson Moses has read Booker T. Washington as being an advocate of self-reliance who contradicts himself by relying on the largesse of the philanthropist. And of course, Lee Walker, my friend, the conservative, also reads self-reliance in Booker T. Washington, and earlier I think Prof. William Allen did as well.

Washington No Conservative

When we interpret Washington's thought on self-help in the context of nineteenth and early twentieth century political vocabularies, the contradiction disappears along with any notion that Washington was a conservative advocate of uplift. The problem arises from the fact that we have not gained a great enough appreciation for what the shift from laissez faire thought to modern thought did for the history of the concepts of self-reliance and self-help.

For those familiar with the language of self-reliance and self-help, there was no contradiction between calling for philanthropic help and self-help – the two went hand in hand. In contrast, in antebellum America, the world of Emerson and Frederick Douglass, self-reliance prohibited the acceptance of philanthropy. The idea of social welfare was virtually unknown. The state helped capitalists alone.

In intellectual combat with conservatives, whites who argued that emancipation would find blacks dependent on whites or philanthropy, Douglass argued that the slaves did not need the support of either the state or philanthropy to survive as free people. During the antebellum period Douglass was incensed at free blacks or even ex-slaves who, when they ran away, found themselves on what Douglass used to call "begging campaigns" – using old white folks' clothes and begging for money. He had no use for those people because they were undercutting his mission of undermining the intellectual underpinnings of slavery. In that golden age of laissez faire capitalism, men were expected to rely on themselves, and virtually no one, liberals or conservatives, thought the state had any duty to assist individuals.

In the late nineteenth century, as the parvenu of the era began to grow a sense of social consciousness, they spawned a new age of philanthropy. That period is not simply called the age of Booker T. Washington. It's also called the age of philanthropy. The state, they believed, had no social responsibility, but those who amassed great fortunes did. They were to be the stewards of society, because everyone – except the true conservatives – was coming to see that interdependence was the wave of the future, that self-reliance could not work in a modern industrial society.

The binary they created by the new age of industrial capitalism was not self-reliance versus self-help, but self-help versus self-reliance. The former binary marked liberal capitalism, and the latter represented the more conservative laissez faire capitalism of the age preceding it. The conservatives were the social Darwinists, who still believed in self-reliance and that any help was bad help.

Changing View of Self-Help

In the late nineteenth century, William Graham Sumner was the leading conservative social scientist of the age. One of his famous essays asked the question, "What do the social classes owe each other?" He opined that social classes owe each other nothing. He was not commenting on social welfare policies of the American state – there were no social welfare policies. He was speaking about what the philanthropists should do with their money.

Now, think about the debate of the Reagan years. During the Reagan years, conservatives said no state help; private help is fine. People can do what they want with their money; if they want to help someone, that's their business. In the late nineteenth century, conservatives said to the philanthropists, don't waste your money on them. Don't even give them private money. So this was a century ago folks, so the language changed.

Self-help did not presuppose that helping people would create dependency. And this is the big problem that all social thinkers have to grapple with: dependency. In different times in history, people have different opinions about what will and what will not create dependency. In our own age, conservatives have told us that any help from the state has a tendency of creating dependency. Not all help – we still give out Pell Grants.

I love going South and arguing to southern conservatives, I agree with you guys, this country is too damn liberal ... I think it all went wrong when they started giving out FHA loans. Then all of a sudden they look at me like I was from the nineteenth century. They believe in certain kinds of state help, because they don't believe that causes dependency. Or, my more cynical friends might say, because they get it. But I don't call anyone's motives into question; I try to take them at their high point.

Competition for Funds

So in the age of philanthropy, the late nineteenth century, self-help was the precondition for assistance, because as long as you had self-help, you would not become dependent on philanthropy. As my grandfather would say – he was raised during that era – you can't help people who don't want to help themselves. But if they want to help themselves, help them.

That was the motto of the great new age of philanthropy of the late nineteenth century.

Whereas self-reliance ruled out aid, the new liberal capitalism piloted by Andrew Carnegie was less afraid of this dependency. Indeed, philanthropy worked precisely because the downtrodden wanted uplift. Washington was no different from DuBois in this. They both believed in self-help. Neither one believed in self-reliance. Some of you folks look at the debate between industrial education and higher education and say, why can't they work together? These ideas are not antithetical. That was a debate about who was going to get the philanthropists' money. Who was going to get Carnegie's money?

That's no high-flown debate. DuBois's position was that higher education was being starved out because vocational education and industrial education were spreading across the land. He wanted Carnegie money to go to Fisk and Howard, or at least Fisk and Howard as well as Tuskegee. Booker T. Washington had no problem with higher education, but he wanted philanthropists to give money primarily to vocational education. They both had their hands out, just like they did a hundred years later. You don't know the history because historians haven't given you this history. They're too busy dismissing people broadly. Washington and DuBois were both advocates of the new philosophy of self-help.

Late Nineteenth Century Conservatism
To get a sense of what conservatism looked like in the late nineteenth century – and I daresay no one in this room is a late nineteenth century conservative, though there are some amongst us in this world – you have to see what Washington was up against. Robert Norrell's work is important precisely because he reads Washington's connection with the true conservatives of his age.

In the South, Washington was dealing with the counterparts of William Graham Sumner. In the North, the issue was often class, but in the South the issue was race. In the North, conservatives opposed public education. There are some who suspect conservatives oppose public education today, but I know not all of them do. In the South, conservatives opposed public education. It was black Reconstruction that bought poor white schools. And when whites built schools in the South, the elite whites built schools for their children. You see, nobody has a problem with dependency for rich people. Poor whites did not have schools. But when schools were built, they had access – better to them than blacks, of course.

The point to be made here is that Southern white conservatives, the white nationalists whom I've studied – and I sometimes look for respectable white nationalists; I have to do that – they really did see blacks as the hewers of wood and the drawers of water. People always used that term. But these folks literally meant it. They understood that blacks had to be illiterate to be pliable. What Booker T. Washington understood is something very simple: If I can get a breathing space, I might be able to flip these guys and throw 'em down. Just give me some space. So my advice to all would-be oppressors – I'll give advice to conservatives too – is, never give an inch. Keep them in the mud. Even a bad school can produce a Martin Luther King.

Washington and Government Support
And this is what Washington understood. And this is why Washington went out to find money from Northerners, because Southern whites would give him no money for education, and only a few whites who were sympathetic

in the South would help. Washington was not against state help. Not just simply taking money from the philanthropists, he'd take money from the state because he had no fear that taking money from the state would automatically lead to dependency. He took money from the state for Tuskegee.

Many of us know the story of George Washington Carver, but what many of us don't know is that George Washington Carver came down to set up an experimental farm. That experimental farm had state money. Booker T. Washington was an advocate of scientific farming, a supporter of the Morrill Act. Many of you today know nothing about this, but the Morrill Act was the greatest intrusion of the state in American life except for the post office. The post office was in every precinct in America, and the agricultural extension service was in every county in America, even in nonagricultural counties.

Conservatives didn't like that. It was a grand intrusion of the state into the day-to-day lives of Americans. It brought you the 4H Club, which still exists – you can't get it out of your life, conservatives say, even where there is no agriculture. In Miami, they have a 4H Club. They probably still have one in Chicago. It has nothing to do with farm life any more. It's the state in your lives. Washington was an advocate of such a use of the state. He believed in state help; he believed in a larger state.

Washington and Assimilation

Just as scholars labeled Washington a conservative – more precisely, just as they misapplied their political vocabularies to define his politics as anti-state – they also misapplied their language to describe him as an assimilationist.

One of the most interesting things about being in this room with a few conservatives is that there is this unspoken disagreement among you about this very issue. Some of you call yourselves conservative multiculturalists, and some of you take the new conservative line, which is to say that there should be a color-blind state and a color-blind society. But Washington was not.

Consider his metaphor of the finger and the hand, in all things purely social. First of all, it is a refutation of the left, who think that most African-Americans had this conflicting "two-ness." Most black Americans were Washingtonians and didn't. But at the same time, if you combine separation that's not state-enforced with the concept of democracy, voila! you have pluralism. Only in America is all separation seen as inherently wrong. But only in America do we have a Constitution that recognized pluralism from the very beginning. Washington was a budding pluralist.

But you say that he didn't believe in black culture, he believed in assimilation. There's something I've never seen quoted by one historian, and it's a quote from Booker T. Washington in an interview with H.G.

Wells. Wells says, "How can you, as a black person, believe in separation?" Washington responded, "Why can't we remain a peculiar people, like the Jews?"

As you may know, in the late nineteenth century and early twentieth century, Jews were a group of people who were thought not to assimilate because they did not want to assimilate. Washington may not have been big on culture, but just like a lot of practical men, that doesn't mean he was against culture. Booker T. Washington's wives were advocates of black culture.

Chapter 21

America and Opportunity

Peter W. Schramm, Ph.D.[23]

I wrote a chapter on Booker T. Washington for a book called *History of American Political Thought*. I've been very interested in Booker T. Washington ever since I was forced to read him at Hollywood High School.

We were in those days forced to read some good books, even at a place like Hollywood High School, which was not exactly the intellectual Mecca of Western civilization, even in 1962, 1963, and 1964, when I attended. But we did read Douglass's autobiography and Booker T. Washington's *Up from Slavery*.

I was born in Hungary and came here in 1956, and as an immigrant it seems to me that my perspective on this is relatively simple, although I hope not simple-minded, and perhaps adds a footnote to Bill Allen's serious, thoughtful, and rhetorically effective articulation of the larger issue.

As an immigrant, I sort of assumed in my bones, one might say, that the reason for being here and trying to become something called an American is that there was some relationship between what one did in one's work and what one kept as a result of one's labor. That's the way my father would have said it, and in fact did say it. And it made perfect sense. It was an opportunity, in other words.

It was an opportunity that was related to what Bill Allen in his indirect way called, "the human thing." Before we left Hungary in the midst of the 1956 revolution, my mother didn't want to leave, because she didn't want to leave her furniture. And my father said that's it, we're getting out of here, the revolution has failed, there's no opportunity for freedom and I refuse to live like a slave anymore.

---

[23] Dr. Peter W. Schramm is executive director of the John M. Ashbrook Center for Public Affairs and a professor of political science at Ashland University.

And so the decision came down to this 10-year-old boy, me. I didn't have a Ph.D. yet, so I wasn't all that smart, as they should've known. But my mother said, we'll leave the country if Peter agrees to leave. So they came to me, and she said, "Are you interested in going with your father; he wants to go far away."

I don't recall this part of the conversation, but my mother does: Apparently I said, with my father I'd be willing to go to hell. Now, let's not get theological about it, but that's a nice thing to say, I think. Having gotten to know my father after all these years, by the way, I'm not sure I would want to go that far. Rest in peace, Dad.

America's Greater Meaning

So the decision was made that we're leaving. And the second part of the conversation, which I do remember, went like this: I said, "Where are we going?" I was smart enough to ask a question.

I should tell you, my father was a window washer – not an educated man, not a professional man or a well-read man. His only claim to fame was that he had been a political prisoner like his father was. His father was a political prisoner because he was a socialist; my father was a political prisoner because he was not a socialist. These are the kinds of regimes you want to avoid.

So I said, where are we going? And my father, this uneducated man, said, "We're going to America." And I said, why are we going to America? And he said, "Because we were born Americans, but in the wrong place." For me of course, that's a very important story. And it's very meaningful for our common deliberative purposes, even though it's personal to me.

America means something to people. You can accept this or not. I don't really care; this is a self-evident truth to me. It's an axiom. It's the beginning of all political conversations, and you don't have to have a political conversation to get there. It's just an assumption that I believe to be true. We were born Americans, but in the wrong place. In other words, we are Americans by nature, even though by convention and by habit and by custom we are not. Which means that somehow, America represents something of this human thing that Bill Allen alluded to for political purposes, that is to say for purposes of freedom.

The American Crucible

Having said that, my point is a very simple one. I get here, and I begin to see things and live in this dreamy world that I've come to know to be America, where I meet people that I think I've met in dreams, where I have teachers named friend, where a teacher forces me to read these black people, Frederick Douglass and Booker T. Washington, and Mark Twain, and I begin to pick up the cadence of the language and the throb of your heart. And I begin to understand what my father meant, in a very practical way. And it moves me, for the rest of my life, to contemplate that meaning.

And most of that contemplation deals with what Booker calls "the American standard" and how those who always appeal to it are the same people who have come through the "severe American crucible." As Ralph Ellison once explained, without these people, many of them former black slaves, America would not be the same. That mixing of the two things, the American standard and the severe American crucible, became the basis of my political and philosophical education.

So you look at the American standard; you look at American, universal principles of rights; you study liberty and equality; and you study why it is that these people – these Americans, at this point admitting to the practice of slavery but not justifying it on some higher moral ground as part of them came to do, say, by the 1830s – why these Americans say that men have a right to govern themselves and then the first thing they do is limit that self-government, limit the power that these human beings have based on equality and liberty under this Constitution. They impose this on themselves to try to get through this object, toward this purpose, toward freedom, to govern themselves – that is, to limit their own power – this is a remarkable achievement. It is a revolutionary achievement in human affairs.

Slavery and the American Idea

At the same time, it goes without saying, certainly in this context, that you have chattel slavery that continues to exist, which they cannot put an end to, even admitting good will, which we don't have to in this conversation, in the Founding period, but certainly admitting necessities, self-interest, and so on. So slavery exists.

However, you now have a standard to which you can appeal in putting an end to it. And in fact that appeal continually is made, and at the same time ironically, perhaps; inexplicably perhaps; but perhaps if we understand the lower aspects of human nature it is not so inexplicable: Those who own slaves begin to justify the ownership of other human beings on the basis of right and racial superiority.

So you look at somebody like Frederick Douglass, who internally makes an argument against slavery that's very practical, that's extraordinarily moving, and makes an argument in favor of freedom and why human beings ought to be free, and then you come to Booker Washington who, although born in slavery, deals with the situation found after Frederick Douglass – he calls it the period of construction and readjustment.

Now the period of liberation is closed, as he puts it, and ironically (perhaps again history works in mysterious ways), Douglass dies the same year that Booker gives the famous Atlanta speech. So Washington replaces him as a leader, and he is now concerned entirely with trying to take a people who have been so manifestly, unjustly enslaved in the worst form of slavery ever devised by man, chattel slavery, and asks himself, "What should we do given that we have been left to our own wiles. What should we do to become free?"

Washington's Courage

This is an extraordinary question that has two components to it. One is how he talks to his own people, in this case specifically the black people, especially the ex-slaves, not people born in the North getting their Ph.D.s from Harvard. He's talking to ex-slaves. And on the other hand, he has to talk to whites in the South because he cannot help but talk to them, even if he doesn't want to. Not just whites, but whites who used to own you. Think about that! Think about the extraordinary difficulty.

So Booker T. Washington is talking to former owners of slaves and trying to persuade them ... of what? Something like, leave us be, let us do our work, and you may hate us less after you see us do good work in the world. And if you don't, it doesn't matter, because then you're hurting your own selves, you white former owners of slaves; you are actually destroying your own souls.

In other words, if we have any doubt about what Booker T. Washington stood for and how much of a man he was – he was a man. Under these circumstances, I would have wilted in a moment.

Think about the courage, the perseverance, the moral virtue that it took to do what he did. He became not just the teacher of his people – of course he was that, and perhaps the greatest teacher of his own people, because he never forgot what the country stood for – he also became the teacher of the white people, who certainly didn't want any teachers.

Confrontation, Not Compromise

Let me quote just two paragraphs from him. He is talking to both whites and blacks, and he says:

> My friends, we are one in this country. The question of the highest citizenship and the complete education of all concerns nearly 10 million of my own people and over 60 million of yours. We rise as you rise; when we fall, you fall. When you are strong we are strong; when we are weak you are weak. There is no power that can separate our destiny. The Negro can afford to be wronged; the white man cannot afford to wrong him. Unjust laws or customs that exist in many places regarding the races injure the white man and inconvenience the Negro. No race can wrong another race simply because it has the power to do so without being permanently injured in morals.

That's a condemnation. And it's not the only place he does it – he does it all the time. In fact, if you think the Atlanta speech is a compromising speech, I defy you to make that argument after you look at the first line of that speech. Instead of saying thanks for having me, a bunch of nice white people, in Atlanta, blah blah blah, instead of saying anything like that, he says, "One-third of the population of the South is of the Negro race."

Whoa! Hardball.

Call for Mutual Generosity

A second quote from Washington, in case you doubt that his educational philosophy struck through any higher level than the unnamed Ph.D. from Harvard would have it:

> But you as white people and we as black people must remember that mere material, visible accumulation alone will not solve our problem, and that education of the white people and of the black people will be a failure unless we keep constantly before us the fact that the final aim of all education, whether industrial or academic, must be that influence which softens the heart and brings to it a spirit of kindness and generosity; that influence which makes us seek the elevation of all men regardless of race or color.

This is a man who wanted to be, and I think became, a teacher of his own people and of white people, of Southern white people – that is to say, of all Americans, even though at the moment and for perhaps two generations we have misunderstood him because he has been forcibly misrepresented, by Harvard Ph.D.s and others.

He always had in mind the promise of America, even though he was living in this severe American crucible. Some accuse him of being an arrogant man. I think he had a lot to be arrogant about.

Chapter 22

Booker T. Washington
and Today's Black Community

Hycel B. Taylor[24]

Let me begin with a quote from the invitation letter sent to me by Lee Walker. He writes, "Booker T. Washington is controversial today because he proves that conservative views played a positive role in the historical black struggle for freedom."

The intent of Lee's statement is to characterize Booker T. Washington as the preeminent historical black conservative, whom Lee believes has a direct correlation to contemporary black conservatives. And I am sure that Lee has researched Booker T. Washington's history far better than I have, to justify such a correlation.

Over the years I have respectfully disagreed with my distinguished colleague merely for the sake of stimulating provocative intellectual debate, and before I discuss the subject I want to begin with a clear and clean definition of the term. The Oxford Dictionary defines conservative in its use as an adjective as follows:

Disliking or opposed to great or sudden change.
Moderate and avoiding extremes.

As a noun, conservative is defined as:

A conservative party.
A conservative person.
A member or supporter of the Conservative Party.
A political party favoring private enterprise and freedom from state control.

---

[24] Rev. Dr. Hycel Taylor is founder and Senior Pastor of The Christian Life Fellowship, a holistic and interdenominational ministry in Skokie, Illinois.

Common-Sense Response

I have serious doubts that Booker T. Washington was consciously trying to conform to any of the above definitions of conservative or any contemporary definition of it. In fact, when he made his historic Rodney King-type "Why can't we all get along" speech to racist white Southern businessmen in Atlanta in 1895, the counsel he used was what he remembered from an old slave woman, which best interprets what seems to be some kind of conservatism, "If you put your head in the Lion's mouth, it's best to pat him a little."

This was not the counsel of a conservative or a liberal, it was the common-sense instruction from a cunning old slave woman who knew how to manipulate and placate the pathological racist sickness of powerful white supremacists. She was wisely aware that the most dangerous white racists would do anything for black folks for a simple pat on the head and allowing them to think they were superior to us.

Well, we still have our heads in the Lion's mouth, and while we don't need to pat him on the head any longer, we should at least let him believe whatever he wants to believe, while we, like Booker T. Washington, concentrate our energies on building our race from the bottom up until we have the power to overpower lions. Presently we are pussycats arguing with lions.

Too long African-Americans have been preoccupied with marching and protesting against lions, appealing to them to help us. Lions don't help people. Lions eat people.

Changing Political Context

This is why I think concepts like "conservative" in the context of this conference would be too controversial if they are taken to imply contemporary connotations of conservative versus liberal or Republican versus Democrat. Too many of us believe George W. Bush is a lion whom we must confront with equal or greater power of lions. Our appreciation and respect for the contributions of Booker T. Washington need not be compromised by such nomenclature controversies. The political agenda of his day was similar to today's political agenda, but not the same.

Also, we should not narrowly define Booker T. Washington as a conservative opposing higher education because of his debates with W.E.B. DuBois on the idea of the talented tenth. Washington made it possible for his own daughter to matriculate at Wellesley College and his son at Fisk University, proudly ensuring they would be among the talented tenth. These controversies should be carefully interpreted within the context of their time.

If indeed this is to be a symposium to reexamine the black agenda, in my judgment what is required is a temporary and strategic suspension of all political and party labels such as conservative, liberal, Democrat, and

Republican. But we should also put aside also all denominational labels of Baptist, Methodist, Catholic, and Lutheran; all civil rights organization labels such as NAACP, SCLC, Urban League, and PUSH; and all fraternity and sorority labels and concentrate on what I think was at the heart of Booker T. Washington's concern for our people: Namely, our common racial survival – how to secure ourselves internally against divisive forces and externally against hostile forces.

Dorothy Sterling and Benjamin Quarles said it best in their book *Lift Every Voice*:

> Washington's moral position was that a Negro should devote his energy to getting where he wanted to go, without caring whether he sat on the front or the back seat. (p. 23)

Need to Be Needed

When considering where we are today as a people, too many of us would rather sit aimless and jobless on a street corner, begging for chump change, than to get where we want to go by doing the menial jobs we used to do, which now undocumented Latinos took over with a strategy to make themselves indispensable to this nation.

To address the question of where are we as a black community today, Samuel Yette said it succinctly in his book written more than 30 years ago, *The Choice*:

> Examination of the problem must begin with a single, overpowering socioeconomic condition in the society: black Americans are obsolete. ... Once an economic asset, they are now considered an economic drag. The wood is all hewn, the water all drawn, the cotton all picked, and the rails reach from coast to coast. The ditches are all dug, the dishes are put away, and only a few shoes remain to be shined. Who needs the Negro?

Sadly, we did not take seriously Sam's counsel 30 years ago when he noted:

> When the decades of the 1970s began, the United States government was officially but unconstitutionally in the midst of two wars: (1) a war of "attrition" (genocide) against the colonized people of Indochina, and (2) an expeditionary "law and order" campaign (repression – selective genocide) against the colonized colored people of the United States.

Now we see that the expeditionary "law and order" campaign (repression – selective genocide) is in full force as they are building mega-prisons to incarcerate us while we are building mega-churches to pacify and console us.

Getting Our Own

Let me hasten to approach the subject given to me, "Booker T. Washington and Today's Black Community," from both a sociological and theological perspective. Let me begin with my sociological perspective.

The speech I am most remembered for when I served as the national president of Operation PUSH in 1985 was titled "Momma May Have, Other Folks May Have, But God Bless Black Folks When They've Got Their Own."

In that speech I took what could be considered a Booker T. Washington position: that while we must continue to protest to get what amounts to crumbs from the master's table – which too often is our primary strategy – it would be far more effective if we would pool some of our money to invest rather than protest.

At that time I was leading hundreds of grassroots black Americans around the country in a protest march against CBS, for which I got myself, Rev. Clay Evans, and others put in jail for breaking into WBBM-TV in Chicago. The meager accomplishment was getting a few procurement contracts and two token positions, one being Lester Holt, who is now a national anchor on TV.

A Day of Dignity and Unity

Since that time, like Booker T. Washington I have been a voice crying in the wilderness, proposing what I believe we as African-Americans can do for ourselves in just one day to dramatically change the course of history. It is an idea I have been proposing for more than 10 years – a national event that would demonstrate in one act the awesome proactive (potential) power of African-Americans: an African-American National Day of Dignity and Unity (Just One Day.) I can see it now as a "Covenant Event" to complement and implement the book edited by Tavis Smiley, *The Covenant*.

It is an idea I proposed in a lecture I gave at Mosque Maryan, which the Honorable Minister Louis Farrakhan acknowledged partly inspired the amazing and magnificent Million Man March. That march and the subsequent "million" marches that were brilliantly led by him could be the preparations for a covenant event in the form of an African-American National Day of Dignity and Unity (Just One Day).

I recently predicted the Latino immigration marches would preempt the "withdrawal from work" concept that I proposed to be one of the key elements of the African-American National Day of Dignity and Unity. But it is still a viable idea because I am proposing an entirely different purpose and end for a covenant event. It is not a singular, massive march, and it is not a reactive demonstration against racism or anything. It is a proactive demonstration of black intra-racial love and unity. However, it would have major consequences for the nation and the world.

Covenant Event

The main elements of a covenant event in the form of an African-American National Day of Dignity and Unity (Just One Day) are as follows:

1. All African-Americans would "covenant" not to go to work (for Just One Day). Rather, we would go to a church, synagogue, mosque, or some secular place to proactively celebrate our blackness and promote the study and implementation of the ideas in Tavis Smiley's book. It could be that a city or rural area would have a united interdenominational and interfaith celebration at a stadium or park.

2. We would covenant to launch a national campaign leading up to that day to commit no crime on that day, no going to prison, no drug dealing or using, no smoking, no rape, no stealing, no drive-by shootings on that day, etc. (Just One Day). We would not get 100 percent participation, but the idea is what is most important.

3. We would covenant to fast on that day (Just One Day) and to bring nonperishable food items to our gathering places to give to the poor and homeless.

4. Most important, on that day (Just One Day) we would covenant to take up a financial offering in every church, synagogue, mosque, or secular place of gathering in the nation and to create an African-American National Endowment for Economic Development (AANEED). The offerings would be called in all day to a national AANEED telethon manned by black celebrities and others. We would also solicit corporations and wealthy individuals to contribute to the endowment. Needless to say, in Just One Day potentially we could create a billion-dollar black endowment. I discuss this idea in greater detail in my book, *The African American Revolt of the Spirit*.

5. Finally, at each venue we would take and sign a sacred covenant vow of commitment to racial dignity and unity.

The course of history is changed by powerful events, either planned or accidental, that alter the way people think about themselves and the world. I think that in the spirit of Booker T. Washington, we cannot wait on an accident. Any catastrophe greater than Katrina, which should have dramatically changed the way we think as a people, will be too late. Instead, we can plan the covenant event.

Chapter 23

Up, You Mighty Nation!

Ishmael Muhammad[25]

I am grateful for the opportunity to reexamine the work and contributions of such a great man – not just an American, but a great human being, a great black man who in his blood had both races, black and white. He was able to offer a viable alternative and a solution, not just for America, but also for the problem that his own black community faced in the early twentieth century.

Our dear theologian, scholar, and freedom fighter, Dr. Hycel B. Taylor, said all of the right things and made the right points, and in truth all I can do is say amen and bear witness to truth. And perhaps strengthen us to honor the legacy of such a great man by doing as Dr. Hycel B. Taylor proposed, and that is that we have to put aside our labels.

We cannot continue to be defined by the labels that have been placed on us, that give to each of us a value but not our true value. I'm neither Baptist nor Presbyterian. I am not Catholic. I am not Jewish. I am not conservative, I'm not liberal. I am a human being – a child of God. I am not American. I'm not African. You cannot define me by geography or territory. I am a child of God.

Washington's Achievement

We are indeed fulfilling what is written in the Scriptures. We are a lost, lost people. I'm representing the honorable Minister Louis Farrakhan, the Nation of Islam, and the honorable Elijah Muhammad. What Booker T. Washington gave, and for which his critics labeled him an "accommodationist," presented something that would have brought black people further along than where we find ourselves today.

Elijah Muhammad advocated that principle of self-reliance, of a people doing something for themselves. Booker T. Washington expressed and

---

[25] Minister Ishmael Muhammad is national assistant to the Honorable Minister Louis Farrakhan.

manifested a spiritual principle that is found in the Koran where Allah says he will never change the condition of a people until that people change their own condition. As a people, we cannot win the respect of others until we show that respect for ourselves. This is why Booker T. Washington won the respect of the white conservatives in the South and they were willing to back him up and did back him up with dollars and money to invest in the building of our own institutions.

Need for Self-Respect

White folks had already told black folks that they were free, but they did not give us the tools by which we could exercise that freedom. However, we had the right to exercise that self-determination which earned the respect of whites in the South during the time of Booker T. Washington and earned the respect of the president during the time that he was invited to the White House. It is this principle, which Dr. Taylor echoed to us, that is sorely missing in our community.

That is why Elijah Muhammad worked 44 years to instill in us as a people self-love, self-respect, and for us not to be a Lazarus at the gate of the rich man begging for crumbs that fall from his table, for you don't see the birds lining up in unemployment lines and you don't see among God's creatures any other creature trying to take the food that is out there for all of the creatures to feed from. The birds are not asking the bees for their honey. And you don't find the lions trying to take what has been given to the birds to eat. How foolish we look, as the honorable Elijah Muhammad said, as a people begging another people to feed and clothe us, to shelter us.

Desegregation has done more harm to us as a people than our effort to integrate and win the hearts of those that oppressed us after they had already given to us our freedom. Self-love and self-respect is the first principle of human nature, and when we show that love and self-respect one to another in the black community, then whites or Chinese or Asians or any other people on this planet will respect black people because we are showing that respect and that love for one another.

Beyond Protest

Dr. Taylor is absolutely correct: The day of protesting and demanding and asking other people to do for us what we can and should and must do for ourselves – those days are over. I don't mind what the conservative whites are doing today. I don't mind that voting rights will come up for review, even though so many of my people paid a tremendous price for us to have that right.

I want you to be careful with that statement; don't take it out of context. The point is that I don't mind them taking back all that they have given to black folks, because if we have failed to take advantage of that as a free people, then let the winds blow on these dry bones that are in a valley, and let these bones come together so they can stand up and take their rightful place in the world. We shouldn't be beggars today, when God has given us so much.

That was the philosophy of Elijah Muhammad, and perhaps he would have been embraced and accepted more by whites in this nation if he hadn't called them devils. But the only reason why he called them devils was to show black people that those who are opposing you are in the character of a devil. A devil is an opponent of what is right and what is good. So he didn't mean it to hurt people or to muddy them. Many whites came out to acknowledge and praise the work of Elijah Muhammad and wished that his work were more alive today, because it is so needed in the black community.

Rights Won, But Identity Lost

As a result of the Civil Rights movement, we achieved the desegregation of the South, and won the right to vote, to drink at white folks' water fountains, to ride in the same bus, and to eat in their restaurants. We won all of that but we lost, because we lost our value and our pride as a people because we have nothing to show and nothing to speak for ourselves.

So a whole generation out there is lost and is now in many traps that have been laid for them. They are filling up the prisons, and they've become disinterested in school, so there's a 70 percent dropout rate. Why? Because our children have lost their values and they can't find themselves any more because the effort to assimilate into America caused us to lose our own identity.

There's nothing wrong with trying to win certain rights – but my God, if you don't come to the table knowing who you are as a child of God, and your place at the table, how can we be respected and honored as an equal member?

We are not American. Not by definition, because to be an American is to be, one, a member not belonging to the aboriginal people. So even in the Constitution, we have to go back and look at the meaning of these words. Otherwise, we are not speaking in the proper terms, and therefore anything that we advance in the people will not go too far, because we are not defining ourselves in a modern context. We are not defining ourselves properly according to the language that we speak.

Need for Washington's Philosophy

I thank those members of the Caucasian community that recognize and see the value of this man for the greater good of America as a whole. But it is sad, Dr. Taylor, to see that we are not here supporting this fully, as though Booker T. Washington did what he did and now that he's gone, and what he offered has no value for blacks today. We need Booker T. Washington's philosophy, and what Elijah Muhammad did in terms of self-reliance, more than at any time in our history. We have more black political elected officials, we have many millionaires, and we even have some billionaires – but what has it meant to the masses of black people? In the words of Louis Farrakhan, "the masses of our people are marching into the oven of social, political, economic, educational deterioration. We are on a death march today."

What is missing, and what we need more than anything, is bringing to the table all of the approaches of Booker T. Washington, W.E.B. DuBois, and Marcus Garvey.

In basketball, you've got to have an inside and an outside game. The goal is to outscore your opponent. And when you have the strong inside presence of a Shaquille O'Neal, it opens up the outside game. The objective is the same: Win the game, and score more baskets than your opponent!

Our problem as a people is that we get ourselves so full of vanity that we separate and distance ourselves from one another, each thinking that our own way is the way. Wait a minute! Let's sit down and take the philosophies, the methodologies, and the approach that you have so that we can work effectively on the inside and on the outside.

Let's work with those white folks to get along. But at the same time, we've got to be developing something within our community, for ourselves. Unless all of us come to the table, none of our demands will be met as a people, because we lack unity, which is the real power of a community of people achieving what they desire.

Up, you mighty nation! We can accomplish what we will.

Chapter 25

A National Apology for Slavery?

William B. Allen[26]

There's a context for talking about the question of a national apology for slavery. I think we have to master what I call the context of this conversation in order to arrive at a clear judgment.

Is this a moral requirement, that the nation apologize for slavery, and would that act put behind us the grievous tensions that we still struggle with, the whole problem of race consciousness? Upon arriving in Michigan in 1993, I was astounded to discover that I was in the most race-conscious place I have ever been and I grew up in the segregated South. That's a reality one really needs to try to factor and think about how this comes to be, what's going on in the country that makes us rivet ourselves so strongly on this question of race.

That invokes the further question of color blindness. And it occurs to me there is a serious misunderstanding about the discussion of color blindness.

Some people imagine there is an argument that conservatives make that says to be color blind means not to acknowledge the reality of color. These are what I call the "race matters" folks. But they're wrong about that.

Color blindness originates, of course, with Justice Harlan and the *Plessy v. Ferguson* dissent – you know that; I'm not telling you anything you don't know. But I want you to understand how Harlan meant it, apart from just the language and the argument.

When we read that opinion, we notice that unlike the majority opinion, Harlan's dissenting opinion used the term "black," unashamedly and consistently. He didn't use any of the euphemisms about race. He was able to make the argument for American citizenship while speaking directly about black people without any phony arguments about community and culture. That said to me something really important. Harlan, the man who

---

[26] Dr. William B. Allen is professor of political science at Michigan State University.

spoke about being color blind, in the very same moment was acknowledging the existence of color.

Race Atheism

What Harlan was trying to tell us is that color blindness doesn't mean there is no color. It means you can see color without seeing a problem. A color-blind world sees a lot of color, but it doesn't see a problem with that color. So the real argument is not the argument about whether color blindness is possible – of course it's possible for serious, morally committed people.

I think the time has come, especially for scholars of these things, finally to say, "Yes, I'm going to embrace color blindness. This is a silly argument. I won't pretend any longer that I've got to argue against the thesis of color blindness. I want to get to the heart of the matter." And that's how we build the context in which to talk about this apology.

I've used another expression to try to describe it: "race atheism." I think this begins to get closer to the nub of the matter. Some of us are race atheists. We really don't think it matters. We don't deny its historical relevance, we acknowledge that. There are many things that have historical relevance that we acknowledge, but there are lots of mistakes in history. There are lots of mistaken judgments, false laws, blind alleys, and improvident decisions. History is a complexity of things often enough that would have been better left undone. To be able to say that, means to be able to evaluate things, to appraise things, their relative standards, their relative excellence.

The race atheists are the people who say, We know why slavery came to be defended by race. We know where the argument for racial inferiority arose. We know it was wrong then. We know it's wrong to try to recapture it now. Are there problems in the society that have to be surmounted? Sure. Can an apology actually surmount those problems? Not, I would submit, if it reinforces wrong judgments about race and color. Not if it lengthens and perpetuates an unnecessary obsession with the question of race.

Sufficient Apologies

One way to illustrate what I mean by calling it an unnecessary obsession is to note that people don't recognize the apology America long ago gave for slavery. That was the apology the famous French philosopher Alexis de Tocqueville could not have imagined.

De Tocqueville predicted America would come to grief in a race war, because there would be no way to settle the question of the three races in America – that was his language, his title for it. What he meant was that he could not foresee what indeed happened, which was the brothers' war. He could not see the enormous shedding of blood over this question, which in the court of Heaven was an apology for slavery – just as Abraham Lincoln told us it was in that second inaugural address. That is where we had a president stand up and tell us, we are apologizing for slavery and God has exacted it from us.

Do we need an apology beyond that, beyond that to which Lincoln has given testimony so eloquently? I don't think so. I think we do need the energy, the moral commitment, the creativity, and the inventiveness, that those gathered here bring to this conversation. I think we need to unleash that power in the broader public discourse, as an instrument to fashion new modes of envisioning community among us. But the secret to envisioning new modes of community is to let go of old impediments to community.

It's very hard, when you're trying to learn to ride a bicycle, to ride without taking one foot off the ground. Children who are learning this always try to sneak that one foot back on the ground; they're always a little uncertain, always a little fearful. But the reality is, if you don't get that foot off the ground, you will not ride the bicycle. And this is a bicycle that we're trying to ride, morally speaking. For that we've got to let go; we've got to get beyond the obsession.

Yes, we scholars are going to talk about it. We're going to keep building the history and retelling the tale. But remember, when we're doing that, we're really engaged in a kind of archiving of the story of our times. That is not the same thing as what, for example, The New Coalition seeks to undertake. They're not interested in archiving. They're interested in building. And there is ample opportunity for that kind of building.

Booker T. Washington was interested in building in this way. That's why Booker T. Washington didn't ask for an apology.

Self-Help and Self-Reliance

I want to urge you to read *The Future of the American Negro*. It's really important to see what Booker T. is saying in that work. He said it elsewhere, also, but he repeats constantly, "I will not surrender even the least of the civil rights promised to us."

For everyone who thought he was an accommodationist, you can't hear him say that and still hold to that argument. For everyone who thought he avoided politics, you can't hear him say that and still believe he avoided politics. He understood that you could cling to the political essence of the community while still addressing the specific needs of a given people within the community, that those were not mutually exclusive terms.

The main point about a proposed apology is simply that it won't do us any good in proportion as we need it. Think about that: That's a deep point. The more we need it, the less good it will do.

With respect to Darryl Scott's distinction between ideas of self-reliance and self-help, I think it important to note that the two terms are not antonyms. I believe this is an accurate account of Booker T. Washington's thinking. What we've got to understand is that there never was in the self-reliance argument an intention to exclude any relationship with philanthropists, because the argument was rather more about self-respect and independence than about the source of resources. Even in the contemporary version, the anti-dependency argument, the argument is more about self-respect, more about dignity, than about the source of the resources people come to make use of.

The claim is that unless people are taking into their own sphere of control the elements of the lives they build, they cannot build worthy lives. It's really that simple. It was true when Booker T. Washington spoke of these things, it remains true now, and it may be the case that although political labels oscillate around these terms, the terms don't change.

I think we should treat self-reliance and self-help as synonyms, rather than as opposites. Those movements, those visions, were only ways of trying to foster the discourse of dignity and self-respect. And everybody believes that the future of community hinges upon the accomplishment of dignity and self-respect.

Liberal Dissatisfaction with America

There is opposition between liberals and conservatives on this score. I described it earlier as the difference between people who believe America works and those who believe that America does not work. Those who believe America can work are willing to be content letting America do what it does, without interfering, while those who believe America cannot work actually want to transform America. And therefore they use the grievances, of blacks in particular, as well as others, wherever possible, in order to foster the argument in favor of transforming America.

But it is reasonable for those who not only believe America works but think there is something important at stake, to say, "Wait a minute, is this transformation that you promise us something that will leave us intact in ways that we desire to remain intact? Or does it put everything at risk?" Does the argument for a little intervention here and a little intervention there not have consequences that we ought to think about in advance?

We know how that debate turned out with respect to public welfare. We saw a system built up that was enormously destructive, and it took a long time before we took the first steps in the direction of reform. That's an important conversation, and numbers are not the index of its importance. I could talk about all the relevant social statistics that tell us we have problems. But from our perspective what matters is not the relevant social statistics, but what we see before us, day by day. That's the decisive evidence for political judgment.

I want to underscore that. Nothing I do professionally ought to influence your judgment about the reality you experience day by day. Your judgment ought always to be superior to my judgment on that question. And the more data I try to put in front of you to coerce you to change your judgment, the more suspicious you ought to be that I'm trying to make you believe that what you see isn't so. In fact, it is so. You've got to learn to trust yourself, just as new mothers have to learn to trust themselves with their new infants, and not to try to nurse with one hand and a book in the other hand.

Earl Warren's Mistake

What growing up means is rediscovering the native powers we bring with us. Earl Warren was wrong in *Brown v. Board of Education*. He was wrong when he wrote those fateful words describing America's blacks as people who, because of the legacy of slavery, were incapable of doing for themselves. Those words are in the legal opinion that we celebrate. We ought to be careful about the celebration.

Yes, segregation was wrong. Yes, it's a blessing that it ended. But remember the opinion that comes with the decision that ends a legal practice has its own viral poison and takes away the blessing of the decision the more we take the viral poison into our bloodstreams.

That viral poison is the belief that the freed slaves could not fend for themselves, that they had to be picked up by someone else, some superior. We've always been struggling to escape this notion that our fate is dependent upon some superior, someone who can do for us what we cannot do for ourselves.

Real Source of Wealth

You've heard me say there is no lack of wealth to solve the many social problems we face, because all that is required to marshal the wealth is to produce it. How simple! That's all it requires. Listen to the statistics about the percentage of the population that owns some percentage of the wealth. It doesn't take a genius to figure out those are wrong, because they are treating as fixed entities things that are not fixed and in a fixed proportion.

Or take the quintile arguments, which are absolutely correct in the discussion of American social mobility. We see less and less movement from one quintile to the next. But then ask the important question: Can you describe the dynamics within the quintiles? Nobody ever does that. Why? Because it's a very confusing picture. This great middle class has done something never before accomplished in human history. It has taken people whom you can call middle class and invested them with enormous wealth, a wealth of such a surprising range that you can leap from the bottom of one quintile to the top of the quintile, never escaping your quintile, and radically alter your circumstances. Thus, you look at a mere middle-class man whose youngsters are better accomplished and better off than he is, and who haven't escaped the quintile.

We've got to become sensitive readers of our picture, of our situation. We've got to understand what it means that we live longer and won't get off the scene, if we want to know how the wealth is being consumed. We've got to understand that the opportunities are not opportunities that await to be awarded to us but instead are constantly present before us.

There is no magic left. There is no little guy behind the curtain pulling the levers. All that's left is us. But I can sing the song of us. I can sing the beauty of us. I can sing the hope of us. I can sing the power of us. We don't need more than us.

Chapter 25

An Apology for Slavery

Carol M. Swain, Ph.D.[27]

It's time for the Republican Party to write a new chapter in race relations. What I have in mind is something beyond the Senate's recent resolution on lynching and this week's expression of regret by a high-ranking Republican official for the GOP's use of what came to be known as the "Southern Strategy." What I propose is a formal apology for slavery and its aftermath. This could take the form of a joint resolution passed by both houses of Congress and signed by the president in a ceremonial setting where Americans could gather to symbolically bury their past.

Whenever the idea of an apology is raised, some whites reflexively recoil. They believe it is a bad idea because it conjures up images of innocent whites prostrating themselves before blacks for crimes they never committed. Most outspoken are whites whose ancestors arrived after the end of slavery and those who fought for the Union. Neither we nor our ancestors, they argue, had anything to do with slavery, so why should we apologize?

Others will say that an apology is not necessary because one has already been issued – two, really. In 1998 President Clinton acknowledged the evils of slavery. And last year President Bush visited Goree Island, a holding place for captured slaves in Africa, and spoke of the wrongs and injustices of slavery. "Small men," he said, "took on the powers and airs of tyrants and masters. Years of unpunished brutality and bullying and rape produced a dullness and hardness of conscience. Christian men and women became blind to the clearest commands of their faith and added hypocrisy to injustice."

---

[27] Dr. Carol M. Swain is professor of political science and professor of law at Vanderbilt University. This essay first appeared in the July 16, 2005 edition of *The Washington Post* and is reprinted here with permission. While this article was not read at the Booker T. Washington Symposium, its inclusion here reflects the ongoing and engaging dialogue at the Symposium between Dr. Swain and Dr. Allen.

That sounds like an apology. Nevertheless, while presidents as far back as John Adams have acknowledged the wrongness of slavery, there is still much to be said for an official apology. It would bring closure and healing to a festering wound.

President Bush is the right man for the job. Since he cannot run for re-election, he can't be accused of pandering for votes. Because he is a born-again Christian, he can and should do this. Since most blacks are Christians, they would graciously accept the apology. By issuing an apology, President Bush could dramatically improve race relations and his party's standing among African-Americans.

A national apology would be a collective response to a past collective injustice, and would imply no culpability on the part of individuals living today. America as a nation would apologize for allowing slavery within its borders, with no individual present-day party being singled out for blame.

Already, our failure to acknowledge such a blatant wrong has set us apart from other great nations that have expressed contrition for misdeeds. Consider Germany, which has apologized for the suffering caused by its actions toward Jews and others. More recently Tony Blair apologized on behalf of Britain for its treatment of the Irish during the potato famine of the 1840s. Pope John Paul II apologized for the past sins of the Roman Catholic Church against non-Catholics. Australia apologized for its mistreatment of the country's aborigine population. What, then, would be the great harm in our apologizing for slavery and the Jim Crow racism that followed?

Opponents will sometimes argue that an apology would open the door to claims for monetary reparations. But a national apology would do no such thing. To begin with, the very legality of slavery before passage of the 13th Amendment would make a claim in tort proceedings highly dubious. Then there is the problem of the statute of limitations having long expired. An additional impediment would be the absence of a living wrongdoer to prosecute. Legal precedent is against it. There is little chance that an apology would trigger the legal liability its opponents claim.

There are no good reasons to oppose a national apology for slavery and plenty of good ones to support it. We would all reap enormous national and international rewards from such a goodwill gesture. The Republican Party would perhaps reap the most. An official apology would offer the party the opportunity to reclaim the mantle of the party of Lincoln by forging a new relationship with African-Americans, one not clouded by the spectacle of Willie Horton or Trent Lott. And it would do immeasurable good in terms of improving race relations. Best of all, it wouldn't cost a cent. That's a pretty good deal all around.

SPEAKER BIOGRAPHIES

WILLIAM B. ALLEN, PH.D. is professor of political science at Michigan State University (MSU). Formerly director of the State Council of Higher Education for Virginia (SCHEV) while on leave from MSU, he served as dean and professor at James Madison College, Michigan State University. He previously taught at Harvey Mudd College in Claremont, California.

Dr. Allen obtained a B.A. at Pepperdine College and a Ph.D. in government at Claremont Graduate School. During his graduate study, he became a Fulbright Fellow, in which role he taught French university students American culture while completing a dissertation on Montesquieu and the American founding.

He served as chairman of the United States Commission on Civil Rights in 1988 and 1989 and was a member from 1987 to 1992. Recognized for excellence in liberal education on the 1997 Templeton Honor Roll (individually and institutionally), he also has been a Kellogg National Fellow and received the international Prix Montesquieu.

IIis newest book is *Habits of Mind: Fostering Access and Excellence in IIigher Education* (with Carol Allen; Transaction Publishers, 2003). He has produced recent studies on higher education, citizenship, Machiavelli, ideas of global community, religious liberty, and other topics.

PETER ASCOLI, PH.D. has been working on a biography of his grandfather, Julius Rosenwald, since 1993. In his business career, Rosenwald is most famous for building Sears Roebuck into America's leading mail order house. But he was also a philanthropist who befriended Booker T. Washington and generously supported Washington's efforts. He spurred the establishment of 25 YMCA-YWCAs to serve African-Americans in cities across the U.S., one of the nation's first low-income housing projects, and more than 5,000 schools for African-American children in Southern states at a time when very few received any public education.

Dr. Ascoli received bachelor's degrees from the University of Chicago and St. Catherine's College, Oxford, and a Ph.D. from the University of California at Berkeley, all in European history. From 1971 to 1978, he was an assistant professor at Utah State University in Logan, Utah. He then moved to Chicago and worked as a fund raiser for a variety of cultural and educational non-profit organizations, including the University of Chicago, Chicago Opera Theater, Steppenwolf Theater Company, and the University of Illinois at Chicago. He also teaches fund raising for the master's degree program in the management of non-profit social service agencies at the Spertus Institute of Jewish Studies in Chicago.

MARK BAUERLEIN, PH.D. is professor of English at Emory University. He is the author of three books: *Literary Criticism, an Autopsy* (University of Pennsylvania

Press, 1997), *The Pragmatic Mind: Explorations in the Psychology of Belief* (Duke University Press, 1997), and *Negrophobia: A Race Riot in Atlanta, 1906* (Encounter Books, 2002).

Dr. Bauerlein received his Ph.D. from the University of California, Los Angeles in 1988.

JOHN SIBLEY BUTLER, PH.D. holds the Gale Chair in Entrepreneurship and Small Business in the Graduate School of Business at the University of Texas at Austin. He is director of the Herb Kelleher Center for Entrepreneurship and director of the Institute for Innovation and Creativity (IC2). His research is in the areas of organizational behavior and entrepreneurship/new ventures/immigrant and minority entrepreneurship.

Dr. Butler has appeared on more than 30 radio and television programs, including Eye On America (CBS Nightly News), The Jim Lehrer News Hour, CBS Radio Talk Show, The Osgood Report, and Public Radio. Also this year Dr. Butler's research has appeared in the *Wall Street Journal, New York Times, Chicago Tribune, Time* magazine, *U.S. News and World Report*, and other newspapers and magazines across America.

His books include *Entrepreneurship and Self-Help Among Black America: A Reconsideration of Race and Economics*; *All That We Can Be: Black Leadership and Racial Integration the Army Way* (with Charles C. Moskos – winner of the Washington Monthly Best Book Award); *Immigrant and Minority Entrepreneurship: The Continuous Rebirth of American Communities* (with George Kozmetsky, forthcoming); and *Forgotten Citations: Studies in Community, Entrepreneurship, and Self-Help Among Black-Americans* (with Patricia Gene Greene and Margaret Johnson, forthcoming).

Dr. Butler received his undergraduate education from Louisiana State University in Baton Rouge and Ph.D. from Northwestern University in Evanston, Illinois.

RALPH CONNER was named public affairs director of The Heartland Institute in April 2005 and government affairs director in April 2006. He devoted the past 20 years to public service for the municipality of Maywood, a community in the western inner-ring suburbs of Chicago. He served as village president (2001-2005), director of planning and development/building commissioner (1990-1995), and enterprise zone administrator (1989-1995). Mr. Conner studied English, journalism, and business administration and marketing at Southern Illinois University and Roosevelt University.

Mr. Conner has been a popular spokesperson for taxpayers, government reform, school choice, and many other issues. He served as chairman of Illinois Public Policy Caucuses (1994), community outreach director of the Illinois Educational Choice Coalition (1991-1992), and a panelist for the Chicago Conservative Conference (2003). He has often appeared as a pundit on Comcast, WTTW, and the Bruce DuMont show.

CHARLES HORNE, PH.D. is president of the Pacific Northwest Chapter of the National Black Chamber of Commerce.

GLENN C. LOURY, PH.D. is the Merton P. Stoltz Professor of Social Sciences at Brown University. He previously served on the faculty of Boston University (1991-2004), where he was founder and director of the Institute on Race and Social Division, and Harvard University (1984-1991), where he was professor of political economy, John F. Kennedy School of Government, and professor of economics and of Afro-American studies, 1982-1984.

Dr. Loury has made scholarly contributions to the fields of welfare economics, game theory, industrial organization, natural resource economics, and the economics of income distribution, and he has presented his research before numerous scholarly meetings and academic societies throughout the world.

He is a frequent commentator on national radio and television, a much sought-after public speaker, and an advisor on social issues to business and political leaders throughout the country. His collection, *One by One, From the Inside Out: Essays and Reviews on Race and Responsibility in America*, won the 1996 American Book Award and the 1996 Christianity Today Book Award.

Dr. Loury received his Ph.D. in economics from Massachusetts Institute of Technology in 1976.

GARY MACDOUGAL chaired the Illinois Governor's Task Force on Human Services Reform from 1993 to 1997. The task force developed and implemented a major reform and reorganization of the state's $10 billion human services system. In his book, *Make a Difference* (St. Martin's Press, 2000, second edition 2005), he shows how Illinois is a model for the nation. He has spoken about welfare reform at forums hosted by The Brookings Institution, Heartland Institute, Heritage Foundation, Hudson Institute, and Manhattan Institute.

Mr. MacDougal is a former trustee of the UCLA Foundation (University of California at Los Angeles), former chairman of the board of trustees of the Russell Sage Foundation (New York), former trustee of the W.T. Grant Foundation (New York), and former director of the Economic Club of Chicago. He served as chairman of the Illinois Republican Party in 2002.

Mr. MacDougal currently serves on the board of United Parcel Service of America and the Casey Foundation (Baltimore). He is a member of the Chicago Club, Harvard Club of New York, Author's Guild, and Council on Foreign Relations in New York.

MINISTER ISHMAEL MUHAMMAD is national assistant to the Hon. Minister Louis Farrakhan and assistant minister at Mosque Maryam, the Nation of Islam's regional and world headquarters in Chicago. He is a son of the Hon. Elijah Muhammad, founder of the Nation of Islam.

ROBERT J. NORRELL, PH.D. is professor of history and holds the Bernadotte Schmitt Chair of Excellence at the University of Tennessee. His expertise lies in Southern history, American history in the twentieth century, and American race relations.

Dr. Norrell earned his B.A., M.A., and Ph.D. at the University of Virginia. He received The Mellon Research Fellowship in American History in 1985 from the University of Cambridge.

In 2005 Dr. Norrell published an interpretive synthesis of race relations in the twentieth century, *United States, The House I Live In: Race in the American Century*. His book *Reaping the Whirlwind: The Civil Rights Movement in Tuskegee* won the Robert F. Kennedy Book Award in 1986. He is the author of 16 scholarly articles and more than 20 encyclopedia articles, and he has written three school textbooks. He is currently at work on a biography of Booker T. Washington.

MARCUS D. POHLMANN, PH.D. is a professor and chairman of the Political Science Department at Rhodes College. He received a B.A. at Cornell College and Ph.D. at Columbia University. He has taught at Bates College, The College of Wooster, Arkansas State University, and Rhodes College. He was chairman of Wooster's Urban Studies Program and directed Arkansas State's Master of Arts in Political Science Program. He also served as a research associate at the Metropolitan Applied Research Center (New York City), as a consultant for Media and Society Seminars (New York City), and was the first political scientist to teach in the former USSR as a Fulbright Senior Lecturer.

Dr. Pohlmann is the author of six books: *African American Political Thought*, six volumes (New York: Routledge Press, 2003); *Landmark Congressional Laws on Civil Rights* (Westport, Conn.: Greenwood Press, 2002); *Racial Politics at the Crossroads* (University of Tennessee, 1996); *Governing the Postindustrial City* (White Plains: Longman, 1992); *Black Politics in Conservative America* (White Plains: Longman, 1990, 1999); and *Political Power in the Postindustrial City* (New York: Stonehill, 1986).

CHRISTOPHER R. REED, PH.D. is professor of history and formerly held the Seymour Logan Chair in North American History at Roosevelt University. A native Chicagoan, he has matched scholarly interest and civic commitment with nativity. He received both his B.A. and M.A. in history at Roosevelt University, and he earned his Ph.D. at Kent State University in 1982. Returning to Roosevelt in 1987 as associate professor, he served as director of the St. Clair Drake Center for African and African American Studies.

Dr. Reed's scholarship includes *"All The World Is Here": The Black Presence at White City*, *The Chicago NAACP and The Rise of Black Professional Leadership, 1910-1966*, and his latest endeavor, *Black Chicago's First Century, Vol. I, 1833-1900* (University of Missouri Press, 2005). Major works in progress include *The West Side of Chicago: African American Life Outside the Black Metropolis*, and continuation of work begun on Vol. II of *Black Chicago's First Century, 1901-1933*.

PETER W. SCHRAMM, PH.D. is executive director of the John M. Ashbrook Center for Public Affairs and a professor of political science at Ashland University. Prior to his work at Ashland, he served in the Reagan administration as director of the Center for International Education in the United States Department of Education.

Dr. Schramm earned his Ph.D. in government from the Claremont Graduate School in 1981. He holds two Master of Arts degrees, one in government from the Claremont Graduate School and the other in international history from the University of London.

Dr. Schramm wrote the introduction to Lord Charnwood's biography of Abraham Lincoln. He has also edited several books, including *Lessons of the Bush Defeat, Consequences of the Clinton Victory*, and he co-edited *Separation of Powers and Good Government*. Dr. Schramm has lectured at The Heritage Foundation, Stanford University, and the International Conservative Congress in Washington, DC.

DARYL SCOTT, PH.D. is professor of history and chairman of the history department at Howard University. He previously taught at Columbia University and University of Florida. He is presently working on a history of white nationalism in the American South and on a study of the displacement of black cotton farmers in Georgia. He is a member of the Executive Council of the Association for the Study of African American Life and History (ASALH). He received his Ph.D. in history from Stanford University and B.A. from Marquette University.

Dr. Scott's book, *Contempt and Pity: Social Policy and the Image of the Black Psyche, 1880-1996* (University of North Carolina Press, 1997) won the Organization of American Historians' 1998 James Rawley Prize for the best work in race relations. He is also the editor of *The Mis-Education of the Negro* by Carter G. Woodson (The ASALH Press, 2005).

Dr. Scott's scholarly work has appeared in numerous journals, including "Postwar Pluralism, Brown v. Board of Education and the Origins of Multiculturalism," *Journal of American History* (June 2004); "The Politics of Pathology," *Journal of Policy History* (Winter 1996); and "Justifying Equality," *Educational Foundations* (Summer 1996).

CAROL M. SWAIN, PH.D. is currently professor of political science and professor of law at Vanderbilt University. In 2003, Dr. Swain founded the Veritas Institute, Inc., a nonprofit organization dedicated to promoting justice and reconciliation among people of different races, ethnicities, faith traditions, and nations.

Dr. Swain received a B.A. from Roanoke College and M.A. from Virginia Polytechnical Institute and State University. She holds a Ph.D. from the University of North Carolina at Chapel Hill and in 2000 was awarded a M.L.S. from Yale Law School.

Dr. Swain is the author of *Black Faces, Black Interests: The Representation of African Americans in Congress* (Cambridge: Harvard University Press, 1993, 1995), named one of seven outstanding academic books of 1994 by Library Choice Council; received the 1994 Woodrow Wilson Prize for the best book published in the United States on government, politics, or international affairs; won the D.B. Hardeman Prize for the best scholarly work on Congress (1994-1995); and was the co-winner of the V.O. Key Award for the best book published on Southern politics.

Dr. Swain's most recent books include *The New White Nationalism in America: Its Challenge to Integration* (Cambridge: Cambridge University Press, 2002), nominated for a Pulitzer Prize, and its edited companion *Contemporary Voices of White Nationalism* (Cambridge: Cambridge University Press, 2003).

REV. HYCEL TAYLOR, PH.D. is founder and senior pastor of The Christian Life Fellowship, a holistic and interdenominational ministry in Skokie, Illinois.

Rev. Taylor was professor of applied theology at Garrett-Evangelical Theological seminary for 15 years. He served as senior pastor for the historic Pilgrim Baptist Church and Second Baptist Church of Evanston. He also served as president of Operation PUSH. He has a Doctorate of Divinity from Vanderbilt University and is an author of *The African-American: Revolt of the Spirit*, published Faith and Freedom Publications in 1991.

LEE H. WALKER is president of The New Coalition for Economic and Social Change and a senior fellow of The Heartland Institute. He is chairman of the Illinois State Advisory Committee to the U.S. Commission on Civil Rights. He is a director of the Black United Fund of Illinois and the Gidwitz Center for Urban Policy at National Louis University, and chairman of the board of the American Fund and trustee of the Foundation Board for the University of the Orange Free State (South Africa).

Mr. Walker is a member of the editorial board and an editorial writer for the *Chicago Defender* and a former monthly columnist for *Crain's Chicago Business*. He is a member of Sigma Pi Phi, Delta Alpha Boulé (Northern Illinois), Chicago Chapter of National Guardsmen Inc., and Chicago Chapter of the National Black Journalists. In 2001 he received the Pioneer Award from the Republican National Committee. He was the 2002 National President of the National Guardsmen Inc. He is listed in *Who's Who Among Black Americans*.

Mr. Walker graduated from Fordham University, New York City, majoring in economics, with additional studies at the University of Chicago, New York University, Brooklyn College, and Alabama State University. In 1975, Walker was elected vice president of the Brooklyn, New York chapter of the NAACP. He worked for 10 years as director of labor relations for a shopping center management company before joining Sears, Roebuck and Company in 1970. He worked for Sears for 23 years, the first 10 in the New York buying office and the next 13 in the national headquarters in Chicago. Mr. Walker accepted an early retirement offer from Sears in 1993 and since then has worked full-time as president of The New Coalition.

FRANK HAROLD WILSON, PH.D. is associate professor of sociology at the University of Wisconsin at Milwaukee. He earned his Ph.D. from the University of Michigan in 1985. Recent publications include *Race, Class, and the Postindustrial City: William Julius Wilson and the Promise of Sociology*, State University of New York Press, 2004, and "NeoConservatives, Black Conservatives, and the Retreat from Social Justice," in Gayle Tate and Lewis A. Randolph's *Dimensions of Black Conservatism in the United States: Made in America*, New York: St. Martin's Press, 2001.

WILLIAM (BILL) S. WINSTON is founder and pastor of Living Word Christian Center, a 15,000-member church located in Forest Park, Illinois. The church has a broad range of entities including a Bible Training Center, a School of Ministry and Missions, the Joseph Business School, the Forest Park Plaza shopping mall, Living Word Christian Academy, and many others. He also hosts the Believer's Walk of Faith television and radio broadcast, which reaches more than 80 million households nationwide and overseas.

Pastor Winston is also the founder and chairman of the Joseph Center for Business Development, chairman of the Board of New Covenant Community Bank (a bank presently in organization), and president of New Covenant Community Development Corporation, whose mission is to revitalize communities spiritually and economically.

After graduating from Tuskegee Institute, Pastor Winston served for six years as a fighter pilot in the United States Air Force, where he earned The Distinguished Flying Cross, The Air Medal for performance in combat, and Squadron Top Gun Pilot competitions.

After completing his military service, Pastor Winston joined the IBM Corporation as a marketing representative. Before he resigned in 1985 to enter full-time ministry, he was a regional marketing manager in IBM's Midwest Region and was responsible for more than $35 million in sales revenue per year.

ANNE WORTHAM, PH.D. is associate professor of sociology at Illinois State University, where she has taught since 1991. Her scholarship interests are the sociology of culture, the history of ideas, and American political culture. She holds a B.S. degree from Tuskegee University and Ph.D. from Boston College. Prior to entering graduate school in 1977, she was a Peace Corps Volunteer in 1963-1965, and for the next twelve years worked as an editorial researcher for such media organizations as *Esquire* magazine, NBC News' Huntley-Brinkley Report, ABC Radio News, and King Features Syndicate.

Dr. Wortham has taught at Wellesley College, Harvard University's Kennedy School of Government, where she was a John M. Olin Foundation Faculty Fellow, and Washington and Lee University. She has also been a visiting scholar at the Hoover Institution at Stanford University.

She is author of *The Other Side of Racism: A Philosophical Study of Black Race Consciousness* (1981). Her work has appeared in *The Freeman, Reason*, and *The World & I*. Her two-hour conversation with Bill Moyers for his PBS documentary series, "A World of Ideas," is widely distributed as a video recording and the transcript published in his book, *A World of Ideas*. Dr. Wortham is currently developing an anthology of her essays on individualism and conducting research on the critique of Max Weber's theory of capitalism by Austrian economists.